100♀

100 most important Women of the 20th century

Ladies' Home Journal® Books

Des Moines, Iowa

100 most important

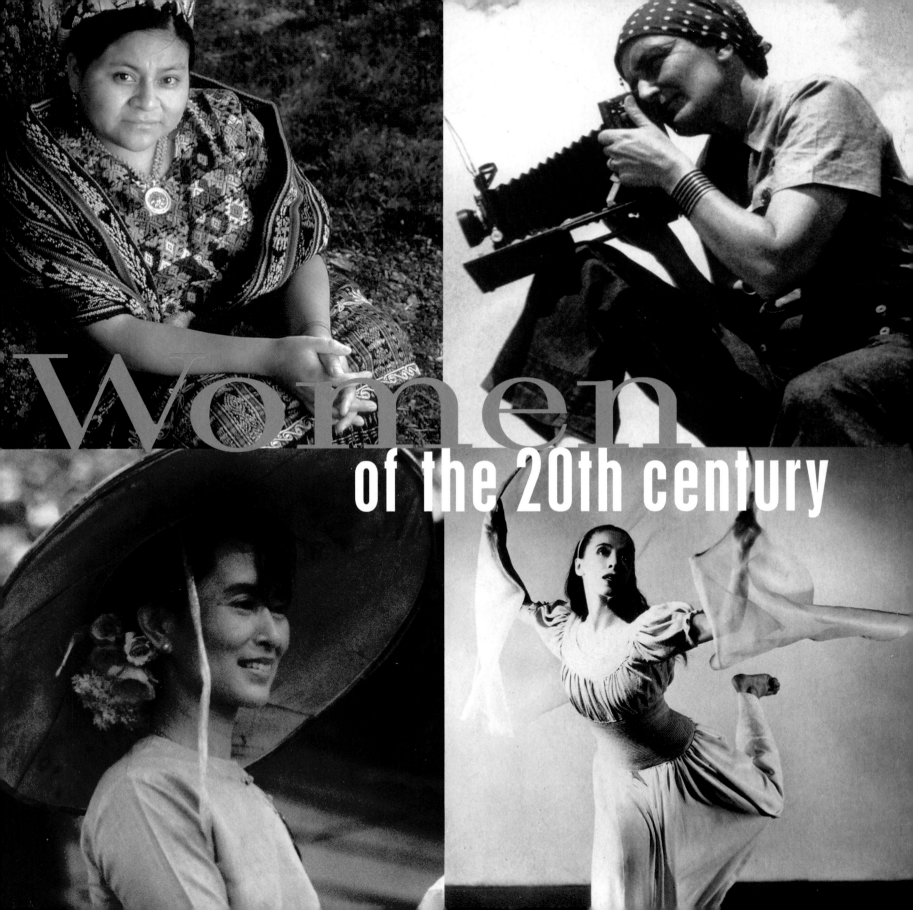

Women
of the 20th century

LADIES' HOME JOURNAL® BOOKS
MEREDITH® BOOKS

Ladies' Home Journal® 100 Most Important Women of the 20th Century

Project Editor: Lorraine Glennon
Author: Kevin Markey
Art Director: Richard Michels
Designer: Stacey Heston
Prototype Designer: Deb Miner
Photo Editor: Laurie Platt Winfrey
Associate Photo Editor: Leslie Mangold
Copy Chief: Catherine Hamrick
Copy and Production Editor: Terri Fredrickson
Contributing Researchers: Peggy Adler, Van Bucher, Jill Benz-Malter, Isadora Fox,
    Susan McDonough, Nicole Micco
Contributing Copy Editor: Becky Danley
Contributing Proofreaders: Sheila Mauck, Debra Morris Smith, JoEllyn Witke
Indexer: Sharon Duffy
Electronic Production Coordinator: Paula Forest
Editorial and Design Assistants: Kaye Chabot, Treesa Landry, Karen Schirm
Production Director: Douglas M. Johnston
Production Manager: Pam Kvitne
Assistant Prepress Manager: Marjorie J. Schenkelberg

MEREDITH® BOOKS

Editor in Chief: James D. Blume
Design Director: Matt Strelecki
Managing Editor: Gregory H. Kayko
Executive Editor: Alice Feinstein

Director, Sales & Marketing, Retail: Michael A. Peterson
Director, Sales & Marketing, Special Markets: Rita McMullen
Director, Sales & Marketing, Home & Garden Center Channel: Ray Wolf
Director, Operations: George A. Susral

Vice President, General Manager: Jamie L. Martin

LADIES' HOME JOURNAL® MAGAZINE

Editor-in-Chief: Myrna Blyth

MEREDITH PUBLISHING GROUP

President, Publishing Group: Christopher M. Little
Vice President, Consumer Marketing & Development: Hal Oringer

MEREDITH CORPORATION

Chairman and Chief Executive Officer: William T. Kerr

Chairman of the Executive Committee: E. T. Meredith III

All of us at Meredith Books are dedicated to providing you with information about women's accomplishments and women's issues. We welcome your comments and suggestions. Write to us at: Meredith Books, Editorial Department, 1716 Locust St., Des Moines, IA 50309-3023.

If you would like to purchase additional copies of any of our books, please check with your local bookstore.

First Edition. Printing Number and Year:
5 4 3 2 1   02 01 00 99 98
Library of Congress Catalog Card Number:
98-66257
ISBN: 0-696-20823-7

most important **100 Women** of the 20th century

Board of Advisors

Jane De Hart

PROFESSOR OF HISTORY

University of California at Santa Barbara

Santa Barbara, California

Ph.D. in History

Anne Fausto-Sterling

PROFESSOR OF MEDICAL SCIENCE

Brown University

Providence, Rhode Island

Ph.D. in Developmental Genetics

Evelyn Brooks Higginbotham

PROFESSOR OF HISTORY AND AFRO-AMERICAN STUDIES

Harvard University

Cambridge, Massachusetts

Ph.D. in History

Linda K. Kerber

MAY BRODBECK PROFESSOR IN THE LIBERAL ARTS

University of Iowa

Iowa City, Iowa

Ph.D. in History

Mary Beth Norton

MARY DONLON ALGER PROFESSOR OF AMERICAN HISTORY

Cornell University

Ithaca, New York

Ph.D. in American History

Vicki Ruiz

PROFESSOR OF HISTORY AND CHICANO STUDIES

Arizona State University

Tempe, Arizona

Ph.D. in History

Anne Firor Scott

W.K. BOYD PROFESSOR OF HISTORY, EMERITA

Duke University

Durham, North Carolina

Ph.D. in History

contents

foreword

by Barbara Walters

Every woman alive
today owes an
immeasurable debt
to the women in
this book.

—Barbara Walters

For women, this has been the most remarkable century in history. If you doubt it, consider for a

moment our status at its dawning. In a world still mired in Victorianism, we were decorative,

disenfranchised, and defined almost entirely by our relationship (be it daughter or wife) with a man.

And that's if we were lucky. ¶ Millions more of us labored under horrific conditions for substandard

wages—sometimes at home, doing piecework; more often in overcrowded textile mills and factories

that put our health in peril. The average female life expectancy? Fifty-one years. ¶ What a difference

a century makes. Today, women's lives have been transformed beyond the wildest imaginings of

someone who lived in 1900. We not only vote and bear arms, we enjoy reproductive freedom and a

large measure of economic equality. We work alongside men in businesses that we've helped build

and that we (sometimes) even own. Thanks to this century's spectacular advances in science and

medicine, we can expect to live at least to the ripe old age of 79. And now, when we ally ourselves

with the opposite sex, it is not out of financial necessity, but genuine desire and love. ¶ *Ladies' Home

Journal 100 Most Important Women of the 20th Century* captures this extraordinary transformation and

celebrates the achievements of the women who helped bring it about. The women profiled here

represent an astonishing range of personalities and endeavors. They are doctors and scientists;

politicians and activists; educators and intellectuals; athletes and entrepreneurs; performers, artists,

journalists, and writers. All have had an influence that is still being felt today and that will endure

well into the next century. ¶ I feel privileged to have interviewed a number of these women—and

even more privileged to be included among them. (I'm actually rather embarrassed, but also

thrilled.) Indeed, my own career may offer an illustration of some of the changes that this book documents. ¶ When I was first hired as a writer on "The Today Show" back in the sixties, television was a murky world of sexism and discrimination against women. I was allowed to write only the so-called soft features for the female member of the cast, then known as the "Today Girl." I could write the script for the fashion shows or a celebrity guest, but never for a segment that dealt with serious news. My big breakthrough came when the executive producer said, "Barbara can write anything the men write." Wow! I was liberated from the tea party. Later, when I was myself the "Today Girl," I went through a period in which the male host (this was not Hugh Downs) insisted that I not be allowed to participate in a hard news interview until he had asked at least the first three questions. Management agreed. That is why, in those early years, I got a reputation for being aggressive (the nice adjective) or, more often, "pushy." You see, if I could arrange my own interview with a newsmaker, and conduct it outside of the studio, I could do the interview. If not, back to waiting until the fourth question at the earliest. The viewers, of course, were aware of none of this. ¶ Finally, after more than 10 years on *Today*, I was given the title of cohost, which is now standard for all the women on network morning programs. But I was not so named until the then-host died and my contract was renegotiated.

I was the first female coanchor of a nightly network news broadcast, but my partner hated the idea of sharing the anchor desk with a woman.

Even when I moved to ABC 21 years ago, the situation was not much better. Sure, I was the first female coanchor of a nightly network news broadcast, but my partner hated the idea of sharing the anchor desk with a woman, and the press reacted as if a major crime had been committed. Oh well, as the saying goes, "how time flies when you're having fun."

Yet, ultimately, that is the point: While I would never say that my career has always been fun, it *has* always been challenging and often enormously satisfying. How could it be otherwise, considering the exceptional people I have encountered? ¶ Many of the women in this book with whom I have talked left their mark by succeeding in a man's world according to men's standards. In this category are Margaret

Many of the women in this book with whom I have talked left their mark by succeeding in a man's world according to men's standards.

Thatcher and Indira Gandhi. Others have exerted a gentler influence. Sublimely funny and sexy, Lucille Ball may not have looked or acted the part of a media mogul, but that's exactly what she was. By speaking publicly of her own health problems to me and others, Betty Ford turned her personal wounds into weapons against drug and alcohol abuse. And a woman I adored talking to, over and over, the incomparable Katharine Hepburn, has inspired all of us by virtue of her stout refusal, ever, to play by anyone's rules but her own. ¶ There are others I wish I had been around to interview. Oh, to have spoken with Marie Curie, Amelia Earhart, or Virginia Woolf! I would have treasured an interview with Eleanor Roosevelt. What a privilege! For years, my fondest hope was of one day talking to Greta Garbo. (I once said I would retire if only she would agree to an interview with me. But then I was afraid she would call up and say, "Promise!") ¶ Every woman alive today owes an immeasurable debt to the women in this book. Without their pioneering accomplishments, I, for one, might never have had the career I have been blessed with, and my daughter's generation would not have the opportunities and choices they now rightly regard as their birthright. As we approach the new millennium, let's look back and pay homage. Then, let's go forward and give thanks.

Introduct

by Myrna Blyth
Editor-In-Chief,
Ladies' Home Journal

The women you see featured in these pages...have made contributions to our culture that influence women today and will continue to influence women's lives well into the coming millennium.

—Myrna Blyth

How do you decide on the 100 most important women of the 20th century? With great difficulty. ¶ After all, this has been a century in which thousands of gifted women in a multitude of disciplines have left an indelible mark on the world. Narrowing the field to a mere 100 women, while an immensely interesting task, was also incredibly daunting. Luckily, the editors of *Ladies' Home Journal* and I had a top-flight group of advisors. They were Jane De Hart, Professor of History at the University of California at Santa Barbara; Anne Fausto-Sterling, Professor of Medical Science at Brown University; Evelyn Brooks Higginbotham, Professor of History and Afro-American Studies at Harvard University; Linda K. Kerber, May Brodbeck Professor in the Liberal Arts at the University of Iowa; Mary Beth Norton, Mary Donlon Alger Professor of American History at Cornell University; Vicki Ruiz, Professor of History and Chicano Studies at Arizona State University; and Anne Firor Scott, W.K. Boyd Professor of History, Emerita, at Duke University. ¶ This distinguished panel of professors helped compile a master list of names (at one stage, we had over 250), which we then whittled down to about 150. *That's* when the process got really tough. We had some spirited discussions along the way, but in the end, there was agreement that the women you see featured in these pages are the 100 who best meet our criteria. From Eleanor Roosevelt to Marilyn Monroe, Coco Chanel to Mother Teresa, all have made contributions to our culture that influence women today and will continue to influence women's lives well into the coming millennium. ¶ Nearly all of the women in this book have appeared at some time in the pages of *Ladies' Home Journal*. From its inception in 1883, the *Journal* has been at the center of women's lives, informing, advising, entertaining, and inspiring millions of readers. This century has seen breathtaking changes in the status of women's health, educational achievements, relationships between the sexes, and political and economic power—many of these changes effected by the women profiled here. But if the *Journal* has empowered women to take their rightful place in what used to be called a "man's world," it has also charted the way the world itself has changed. The issues at the heart of the *Journal*—once dismissed as mere "women's concerns"—now dominate our public debate. ¶ At this moment in history, women have more power than ever before—though women themselves are sometimes the last to acknowledge it, or even to feel it. Perhaps that is because, while women may revel in their new strength, their satisfaction is tempered by an awareness that something has been lost, as well. The remarkable women profiled here often found themselves at odds with the prevailing culture, and many paid a high price in their personal lives for their distinctiveness. In their pursuit of the extraordinary, they often had to forgo the ordinary pleasures of marriage and children. Let us hope that in the 21st century the diverse elements of women's lives can at last be integrated, so that women can use *all* of their talents without having to sacrifice any of the traditional definitions of happiness. ¶ Personally, I haven't the slightest doubt that women can accomplish all this and more. If there is one lesson I have learned from these 100 women and from my many years as the editor of *Ladies' Home Journal*, it is this: Never, *ever*, underestimate the power of a woman.

Activists & Politicians

"I've often thought that when something is hard for you, whether it's going to law school or anything else that challenges you, that's probably what you should do."

— Hillary Rodham Clinton

jane **Addams**

> **Old-fashioned ways which no longer apply to changed conditions are a snare in which the feet of women have always become readily entangled.**

1860—1935

AT THE TIME OF HER DEATH, JANE ADDAMS WAS, AS *THE NEW YORK TIMES* WROTE IN HER OBITUARY, "PERHAPS THE WORLD'S BEST-KNOWN AND BEST-LOVED WOMAN." ¶ TODAY, ADDAMS MAY NO LONGER BE A household name, but the legacy of her good works can still be felt in every corner of American society. In fact, her ideals may well be more relevant now than they were a century ago. ¶ Consider, for instance, the best-known piece of that legacy—Chicago's Hull House, the crowning achievement of the turn-of-the-century settlement house movement. The precursors of modern social service agencies, settlement houses were designed and run (often by college-educated women) to help immigrants adjust to life in the United States by offering job training, medical services, education, child care, and cultural programs in their own neighborhoods. This community-based approach to solving social problems has recently been rediscovered; when today's citizens are urged to "think globally, act locally," they are hearing a message that Addams lived. ¶ Addams and her old college friend Ellen Gates Starr purchased Hull House, a once-stately mansion in one of Chicago's most rundown immigrant neighborhoods, in 1889. Soon, it was offering assistance to tens of thousands of people a year. Addams not only lived at Hull House (which eventually included 13 buildings and a rural summer camp), she was intimately involved in its daily management. With the aid of an exceptionally talented (and mostly female) staff, she opened its parlor to a group of union women for their meetings, built a playground, a gymnasium, and a day-care facility, and arranged housing for women and children facing homelessness in the aftermath of factory layoffs or strikes. ¶ Somehow, Addams also found time to write several books and to campaign on behalf of causes ranging from child labor to racial equality to women's suffrage. She was on the executive council of the National Association for the Advancement of Colored People at its founding in 1909. In 1920, she helped create the American Civil Liberties Union. But her greatest passion was peace, and in 1931 this lifelong pacifist became the first American woman to win a Nobel. In awarding her the peace prize, the Nobel committee called Addams "the foremost woman of her nation."

madeleine
Albright

U.S. Secretary of State Madeleine Albright greets Palestinian leader Yassar Arafat prior to the start of 1997 talks aimed at restarting the Middle East peace process.

1937—

"WOMEN'S CAREERS DON'T GO IN STRAIGHT PATHS," MADELEINE ALBRIGHT ONCE SAID. "THEY ZIGZAG ALL OVER THE PLACE." AS THE FIRST WOMAN to achieve the pinnacle of international diplomacy— U.S. Secretary of State—Albright is a perfect demonstration of her own thesis. ¶ Born Madeleine Korbel in Prague shortly before Hitler invaded Czechoslovakia, Albright and her family (whom she believed to be Catholic until 1997, when newly unearthed information revealed that they were Jewish) escaped to England during the war. After the Allied victory, they returned briefly to Czechoslovakia but were forced to flee again when the country was overrun by the Soviet Union. Albright was 11 when the family settled in Colorado. ¶ College—she attended Wellesley on a scholarship—was quickly followed by marriage (to publishing heir Joseph Albright), then motherhood. Albright was in her thirties when she began working on her Ph.D. in international affairs at Columbia University, studying late into the night after her three daughters were in bed. In 1977, when her doctoral advisor, Zbigniew Brzezinski, became head of the National Security Council, he tapped Albright for a staff job. ¶ Albright's world was rocked once again in 1982, when her husband of 23 years left her for another woman. Devastated, she set about transforming herself into a political heavyweight—teaching government at Georgetown University, advising Democratic presidential contenders, and hosting foreign policy discussions in her Washington home. As a survivor of both Nazi and Communist invasions, Albright did not shrink from the idea of using military force against international aggressors. ¶ By the time Bill Clinton became president in 1993, Albright was a natural choice for U.N. ambassador. Four years later, it seemed just as natural that the President should name her the first female Secretary of State. "She watched her world fall apart," said Clinton. "And ever since, she has dedicated her life to spreading to the rest of the world the freedom and tolerance her family found in America."

66

I have very set

and consistent

principles,

but I am flexible

on tactics.

I like to get the

job done.

99

m a r y   m c l e o d

Bethune

Invest in the human soul. Who knows, it might be a diamond in the rough.

1875—1955 IF ALL WOMEN FACED TREMENDOUS OBSTACLES TO ADVANCEMENT IN THE OPENLY DISCRIMINATORY TURN-OF-THE-CENTURY UNITED STATES, AFRICAN-AMERICAN WOMEN BORN TO FORMER slaves and living in the South faced a nearly impenetrable wall. By virtue of talent, determination, and absolute faith in her principles, one such daughter of slaves, Mary McLeod Bethune, went on to become the most powerful black woman ever to serve in the American government. She also became an inspiration to thousands—female and male, black and white. ¶ Devoutly religious and passionate about education, Bethune won a scholarship to what later became Chicago's Moody Bible Institute, where she was the only black student. She taught in black elementary schools in the South for several years, then, after separating from her husband, moved with her young son to Florida in 1904. Although its burgeoning resort economy attracted many black workers, Daytona Beach, like most southern cities, excluded minorities from its public schools. Selling homemade potato pies to local workmen, Bethune raised $5 for a down payment on a four-room cottage that she furnished with scavenged packing crates and opened as the Daytona Normal and Industrial Institute, a private school for African-American girls (tuition was 50 cents a week; no student was turned away). It merged with Cookman Institute for Men in 1923, becoming Bethune-Cookman College—to this day one of the country's leading black colleges. ¶ Bethune's friendship with Eleanor Roosevelt, one of the school's benefactors and a leading champion of civil rights, led to Bethune's most notable accomplishment—becoming the first black woman to head a federal agency. In 1936, FDR appointed her director of Negro Affairs for the National Youth Administration. Eager to promote civil rights from within government, Bethune, using her abundant charisma and political shrewdness, assembled 30 blacks from the alphabet-soup agencies of the New Deal into the Federal Council on Negro Affairs. Among the many achievements of this "black cabinet" was the creation of the Fair Employment Practices Commission.

1859—1947

THE RIGHT TO VOTE. IT IS THE MOST FUNDAMENTAL ELEMENT OF A WORKING DEMOCRACY. AND YET, UNTIL 1920, SOME 144 YEARS AFTER THE BIRTH OF the republic, it was denied to half of America's adult population. Without the ceaseless efforts of Carrie Chapman Catt, the wait would have been even longer. ¶ Until Catt masterminded the strategy that got the 19th Amendment ratified, female suffrage was widely written off as a quixotic pursuit with little likelihood of success. Deftly shifting the movement's focus from mere consciousness-raising to nuts-and-bolts political action, Catt, as president of the National American Woman Suffrage Alliance, organized NAWSA's district committees in 36 states to apply local pressure to get state legislatures to pass the amendment. ¶ Although Catt had been interested in women's equality since college, it was not until the untimely death of her husband, Leo Chapman, owner and editor of the *Mason City* [Iowa] *Republican*, in 1886, that she became consumed with the issue of suffrage. She joined the Iowa Woman Suffrage Association, and in 1890 attended the first annual conference of the newly formed NAWSA, where she quickly proved herself indispensable to the cause. Personable, good-looking, and energetic, she was one of the movement's most persuasive speechmakers and gifted administrators. ¶ Widowed for a second time in 1905—she had married the prosperous, liberal-minded construction owner George Catt 15 years earlier—Catt was left financially secure and free to pursue her crusade full-time. ¶ After seeing her dream finally realized, Catt turned her attention to the cause of world peace. She also worked to educate the newly enfranchised American woman. The right to vote was not enough, she asserted: It must be exercised wisely. Accordingly, in 1919 she formed the League of Women Voters, to this day one of the country's preeminent nonpartisan voter education groups.

> **66**
>
> Woman
>
> suffrage
>
> is a long story
>
> of hard work
>
> and heartache,
>
> crowned
>
> by victory.
>
> **99**

carrie chapman

Catt

hillary rodham
Clinton

> **Our global future depends on the willingness of every nation to invest in its people, especially women and children.**

1947—

HILLARY RODHAM CLINTON'S ARRIVAL IN THE WHITE HOUSE IN 1993 MARKED A NEW ERA IN PRESIDENTIAL HISTORY: FOR THE FIRST TIME, THE PRESIDENT'S SPOUSE WAS NOT A CAREER WIFE, BUT A CAREER WOMAN. STEPPING INTO THE ROLE OF FIRST LADY—A VAGUELY defined, unpaid position with almost no clear-cut official duties—Clinton struggled to make her mark while enduring near-constant scrutiny from the press and a fascinated public. ¶ Like Eleanor Roosevelt, Clinton was dedicated to public service long before moving into the White House. Once there, she used her prominence and her own experience as a modern working mom to promote women's and children's rights. Like Roosevelt as well, she exhibited grace under pressure and a fierce loyalty to her husband, even as his perceived philandering cast her in the awkward position of wronged wife. ¶ Raised in a conservative Chicago family, Hillary Rodham was a high achiever from childhood. Valedictorian of her 1969 class at Wellesley College, she went on to Yale Law School. In 1973, she came to Washington to help Marian Wright Edelman, founder of the Children's Defense Fund, gain new legislative protections for children.

After marrying Bill Clinton in 1975, she entered private legal practice in Arkansas, becoming her firm's first female partner. In 1980, she gave birth to daughter Chelsea. ¶ Shortly after winning the presidency in 1992, Bill Clinton named his wife to the monumental job of heading up a National Health Care Task Force. Her committee's complex proposals never became law, but they did contribute to a breakthrough acknowledgment that the health care system was flawed. ¶ Although the Clinton White House has been beset by scandals, Hillary Clinton's reputation as a social reformer is unassailable. "The trouble is," said political biographer Carl Sferrazza Anthony in *Ladies' Home Journal*, "she's a century ahead of her time."

> The legacy
> I want to leave
> is a child-care
> system that says
> that no kid
> is going to be
> left alone
> or left unsafe.

1939—

FOR 25 YEARS MARIAN WRIGHT EDELMAN HAS BEEN LEADING A SOMETIMES QUIXOTIC, ALWAYS passionate crusade to improve the lives of America's most vulnerable citizens. Founder and president of the Children's Defense Fund, Edelman awakened Americans to the fact that children have rights, too. She has done more to shape national policy on such issues as infant mortality, day care, child abuse, and teenage pregnancy than probably any legislator who has ever worked in Washington. And she has done it without benefit of elective office. ¶ In place of vested political power, Edelman, a Yale-trained attorney, relies on hard work, an insider's knowledge of how the system works, and profound faith in her mission. "You really *can* change the world," she once told *Ladies' Home Journal,* "if you care enough." Care she does. Growing up the daughter of a Baptist minister in segregated Bennettsville, South Carolina, Edelman was drilled in basic Christian virtues. "Working for the community was as much a part of our existence as eating and sleeping," she recalls. ¶ That commitment to community service never flagged. Upon receiving her law degree in 1963, Edelman returned south to work for the NAACP on the way to becoming the first African-American woman ever admitted to the Mississippi bar. In 1968, deciding that the quickest route to social change was from the top down, she moved to Washington and started the Washington Public Policy Research Center, a major civil rights advocacy group. ¶ With marriage (to Peter Edelman, an assistant secretary at the U.S. Department of Health and Human Services during the first Clinton Administration) and motherhood (three sons, who "always came before career"), Edelman's focus shifted. "The children—my own and other people's—became the passion of my personal and professional life," she said. Since its inception in 1973, the Children's Defense Fund has served as the chief federal advocate of the rights of children—to safe homes, nutritious meals, and decent educations. So powerful is Edelman's role as a leading Congressional adviser on family issues that she has been called "the 101st Senator."

marian wright
Edelman

indira Gandhi

1917—1984 INDIRA GANDHI WAS THE PERSONIFICATION OF MODERN INDIA. FOR NEARLY TWO DECADES, THIS "idealist without illusion," as she has been called, held the world's largest, and most fractious, democracy together, attempting to steer it out of the morass of third-world poverty. ¶ The Oxford-educated, fiercely patriotic daughter of Jawaharlal Nehru, postcolonial India's founder and first prime minister, Gandhi (her married name; no relation to the Mahatma) cut her teeth on India's independence movement. Her earliest political act, at age four, was to throw her favorite doll (an English import) into a bonfire as part of a boycott of European goods. She was elevated to the post of prime minister in 1966 by the power brokers of the Indian National Congress, the political party she headed, partly on the assumption that she was a "dumb doll" who would do as they said. Instead, they discovered a shrewd politician. During her first term, she led India to victory in a 1971 war against Pakistan, gave diplomatic recognition to Bangladesh (formerly East Pakistan), and launched a program to eradicate poverty. ¶ Poverty proved stubbornly resistant to eradication, but Gandhi was reelected by a landslide in 1972. Three years later, she was indicted for fraud and barred from office. She struck back by declaring a state of emergency, suspending the courts, muzzling newspapers, and eventually having some 20,000 political opponents arrested. When she finally restored civil liberties in 1977, she was immediately voted out of office, only to be reinstated in 1980. For better or worse, the electorate seemed to say, Gandhi was destined to be their leader. ¶ But Gandhi herself fell victim to the violent sectarianism she despised. In June 1984, when Sikh extremists from the secessionist Punjab state occupied the sacred Golden Temple at Amritsar, she sent in the army. Some 450 Sikhs were slaughtered. Their brutal retaliation came in October, when two Sikh members of Gandhi's personal security detail gunned down the prime minister in her private garden. ¶ "I don't mind if my life goes in the service of the nation," she once said. "If I die, every drop of my blood will invigorate the nation."

[*Indira Gandhi was known to her supporters as Mother India. Her father, Jawaharlal Nehru (above with Gandhi in 1956) was the country's first prime minister.*]

> **66**
>
> **My father was a statesman; I'm a political woman. My father was a saint; I'm not.**
>
> **99**

ACTIVISTS & POLITICIANS

1933—

RUTH BADER GINSBURG FUNDAMENTALLY ALTERED THE SUPREME COURT BY BRINGING TO IT A 1990S VOICE OF PRAGMATIC, MAINSTREAM FEMINISM. THE SECOND WOMAN EVER APPOINTED TO THE NATION'S HIGHEST JUDICIAL BODY, Ginsburg has made a career—as professor, women's rights advocate, appellate court judge, and finally Supreme Court justice—of ensuring that women receive equal treatment under the law. ¶ Ginsburg was spurred toward her role as a crusader for women's equality by the discrimination she experienced in her own career. After graduating from Columbia University Law School, where she made Law Review and tied for number one in the class, she watched top firms gobble up her male classmates. Meanwhile, she received not a single offer. "I had three strikes against me," she later wrote. "I was Jewish and the firms were just opening up to Jewish students. I was a woman. And I was a mother [her first daughter was born before she entered law school]." She was also turned down for a clerkship with Supreme Court Justice Felix Frankfurter, who told her he was not ready to hire a woman. She ended up clerking for a federal judge in New York. ¶ During the 1970s, as director of the American Civil Liberties Union's Women's Rights Project, Ginsburg argued six landmark discrimination cases before the Supreme Court, winning five. Her advocacy led the Court to strike down a range of federal and state laws that granted privileges based on sex. Yet Ginsburg has been a remarkably restrained judge. Upon being named to the Federal Court of Appeals in 1980, Ginsburg did not pursue sweeping social change, as some observers predicted, but became a pragmatic jurist who valued real-world experience over political ideology. Her record earned her the respect of conservative lawmakers, and when President Clinton tapped her for the Supreme Court in 1993, the Senate approved her nomination 96 to 3. "It is essential to a woman's equality with man that she be the decision-maker," she told the Senate Judiciary Committee. "If you impose restraints, you are disadvantaging her because of her sex." Because of jurists like Ginsburg, such disadvantages are becoming a thing of the past.

> " I don't think there would have been a chance for the laws against sex discrimination if women had not begun to come alive and agitate for increased rights and opportunities. "

r u t h   b a d e r
Ginsburg

26

e m m a Goldman

> Demand work.
>
> If they do not
>
> give you work,
>
> demand bread.
>
> If they deny
>
> you both,
>
> take the bread.
>
> It is your
>
> sacred right.

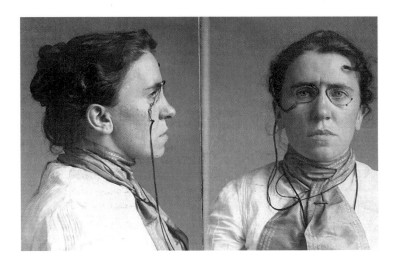

1869—1940

A REBEL AND A RABBLE-ROUSER IN THE CLASSIC, 19TH-CENTURY MODE, Emma Goldman was the prototype for the political radicals of the 1960s. Red Emma, as she was known to friend and foe alike, railed against inequality wherever she found it. And in the early years of the American century, she found it almost everywhere. ¶ Born in what is now eastern Lithuania, Goldman emigrated to America to escape an arranged marriage. Any romantic notions about the American dream quickly evaporated, however, after she went to work as a seamstress in a Rochester, New York, sweatshop for $2.50 a week—an experience that permanently soured her on capitalism. ¶ After moving to New York City in 1889, Goldman met some of the key figures in the American anarchist movement and committed herself to "a new social order based on liberty unrestricted by man-made law." In 1892 she was implicated (though not formally charged) in a failed attempt on the life of Carnegie Steel millionaire Henry Clay Frick. She did serve a year in prison, however, for inciting unemployed workers to riot.¶ By the early 1900s, Goldman had renounced violence, but she continued to agitate and thus remained an enemy of the U.S. government. In 1905, she cofounded the radical journal *Mother Earth,* a clearinghouse of information on topics ranging from workers' rights and freedom of speech to women's emancipation and "free love," by which she meant freedom from legal encumbrances. ¶ Goldman went to prison a second time for opposing military conscription during World War I; upon her release in 1919, she was deported to Russia, where she surprised other radicals by being as critical of Lenin's Communist regime as she was of capitalism. ¶ In her own era, Goldman was too prickly, too uncompromising, to be widely accepted. Only in the years since her death has her spirited defense of liberty in all its guises been accorded the admiration it deserves.

anita Hill

> **It is only after a great deal of agonizing, consideration, and sleepless nights that I am able to talk of these unpleasant matters to anyone but my closest friends.**

1956— LIKE THE ARMY-MCCARTHY HEARINGS OF THE 1950S OR THE ASSASSINATION OF JOHN F. KENNEDY, LAW PROFESSOR ANITA HILL'S DISTURBING 1991 accusation of sexual harassment against her former boss, Supreme Court nominee Clarence Thomas, became a defining moment in America's social history. Never before had the explosive issue of women's treatment in the modern workplace been aired so openly. Never again could it be blithely ignored. ¶ Hill had made her charges confidentially to the Senate Judiciary Committee overseeing Thomas's confirmation. Only after the story was leaked to major news media did she reluctantly agree to go public. As millions of American households tuned in to watch, Hill testified before the all-white, all-male committee that the would-be justice had engaged in inappropriate and suggestive behavior to her during his tenure as head of the Equal Employment Opportunity Commission (the federal agency responsible for investigating sexual and other forms of discrimination). Thomas, his former aide maintained, had repeatedly pressured her for dates, boasted of his sexual prowess, and subjected her to lewd comments. Thomas (like Hill, an African-American) categorically denied all charges, going so far as to call the confirmation process a "high-tech lynching." ¶ The Senate ended up confirming Thomas by a 52-48 vote (though not before his sponsors in Congress had characterized the shy, prim professor as everything from a golddigger to a bitter old maid), but opinion polls taken a year later told another story: More Americans, especially women, believed her than him. A deepening sense that men "just don't get it" spurred a record number of women to run for, and win, public office, making 1992 the "year of the woman" in American politics. ¶ But Hill's most fundamental contribution may have been to get Americans talking about what goes on between men and women at work. "I thought sexual harassment was if you touched someone," one young man told *Time* magazine. Thanks to Anita Hill, such lack of awareness can no longer be excused.

[*The nation sat transfixed during the 1991 Senate Judiciary Committee hearings on the appointment of Supreme Court nominee Clarence Thomas.*]

dolores

Huerta

1930— AS COFOUNDER, FIRST ELECTED VICE PRESIDENT, AND PRINCIPAL NEGOTIATOR OF THE UNITED FARM WORKERS UNION, Mexican-American labor organizer Dolores Huerta has dedicated her life to gaining equal economic, political, and social rights for the poorest of America's working poor and the last large group of laborers to be organized—its migrant farmhands. Along the way she showed that women had a crucial role in every part of the labor movement, including in its smoky back rooms and on its often brutal front lines. ¶ As second-in-command to the UFW's legendary cofounder, César Chavez ("we were close," she has said, "because I was the only person he met who was as fanatical as he was"), Huerta in the 1960s and '70s organized the UFW's landmark boycotts against California's largest growers of lettuce and table grapes. Consumers were urged not to buy those foods until farm workers' grievances—subsistence pay, lack of medical benefits, unsanitary housing, and work environments made toxic by pesticides, among other complaints—were redressed. ¶ Huerta was arrested some 20 times, went to jail, and was beaten by hired union busters. When the boycott succeeded, she negotiated the union's first contract with the growers. She also helped to establish the first credit union for farm workers and to secure minimum wage guarantees, pensions, and unemployment and disability insurance for Mexican farm workers, regardless of citizenship. ¶ Huerta's toughness and unwavering commitment to nonviolence helped turn *La Causa*, as the movement was called, into a family affair. She brought her children with her to the picket lines, and other women followed her lead. Their presence, Huerta believed, drove home the point that "when we're talking about benefits and the terms of a contract, we're talking about families." ¶ Over the years, Huerta expanded La Causa's scope to include the basic civil freedoms of all Latinos in the United States. Indeed, her famous phrase—"¡Sí, se puede!" ("Yes, we can!")—has become the rallying cry of the entire Latino civil-rights movement.

> Brother,
>
> I am not asking
>
> for the moon for
>
> the farm workers.
>
> All we want
>
> is just a little
>
> ray of sunshine
>
> for them!

ON THE OCCASION OF HER RETIREMENT IN 1970, MAGGIE KUHN, A 25-YEAR EMPLOYEE OF THE UNITED PRESBYTERIAN CHURCH IN NEW YORK CITY, WAS PRESENTED WITH A SEWING MACHINE. "I never opened it," she said later. "I was too busy." As the sewing machine collected dust, Kuhn, hopping mad at being forced to leave a job solely because she had hit the arbitrary cutoff age of 65, launched the public advocacy group known as the Gray Panthers (a witty variation on the name of the Black Panthers, a radical black organization she admired). With it, she helped create a worldwide awareness of what she called "ageism."

It is morally wrong, she declared, to throw people on the scrap pile just because they are no longer young—and no less a social evil than racism or sexism. ¶ Under Kuhn's energetic leadership, the Gray Panthers grew to a peak membership of 60,000—and eventually helped rewrite mandatory retirement laws. But unlike such organizations as the powerful American Association of Retired Persons, the Gray Panthers were always about more than elderly issues. Kuhn's tireless muck-raking on behalf of causes as disparate as the antiwar movement and national health care galvanized activists of all ages and backgrounds, so that during the Gray Panthers' early-1980s peak almost 40 percent of its membership was younger than 50. ¶ Kuhn's personal life was as unorthodox as her public career. Twice engaged but never married ("sheer luck," she liked to quip), she maintained that she never regretted her decision to remain single. "If I had married them," she said of her suitors, "my life would have been over." As it was, she had numerous love affairs, including one when she was in her 70s with a man less than half her age. "We may get old," Kuhn told a reporter, quoting Congressman Claude Pepper, a friend and longtime patron of the elderly, "but we still get hot." For such freethinking, as well as for her superior political skills and dedication to social justice, Kuhn remains a model of ageless liberation.

> 66
>
> **There's no disgrace or shame in growing old. We're all doing it.**
>
> 99

maggie **Kuhn**

g o l d a
Meir

1898 — 1978 GOLDA MEIR IS ONE OF THOSE MONUMENTAL POLITICAL FIGURES WHO IN THE POPULAR IMAGINATION COMES TO SYMBOLIZE AN ENTIRE NATION. ISRAEL'S FOURTH PRIME MINISTER AND THE ONLY WOMAN TO DATE TO HOLD THAT OFFICE, MEIR DEDICATED VIRTUALLY HER ENTIRE ADULT LIFE TO her country's survival and advancement. Small wonder that she is known as "Mother Israel." ¶ Born Golda Mabovitch in Kiev, Ukraine, Meir moved to the United States with her family in 1906. She married Morris Myerson, who shared her budding interest in the Zionist labor movement, in 1917, and four years later the couple emigrated to Palestine. In the years following World War II, as Palestine became a British mandate, Meir was a masterful fund-raiser for the Zionist cause, combining an eloquent speaking style, a warm, "chicken-soup"-style maternalism, and an absolutely unshakable commitment to Zionism. In May 1948, she was one of the signers of the Israeli Declaration of Independence. She held a variety of high posts in the new government of Israel's first Prime Minister David Ben-Gurion, eventually becoming foreign minister. When Ben-Gurion asked his cabinet to adopt Hebrew names, Myerson, whose marriage ended in 1941, became Meir, which means "illuminate." ¶ Meir became Prime Minister of a Labor Party government in 1969 when she was asked to fill in after the death of the incumbent Levi Eshkol. She was elected in her own right later that year. As Prime Minister, Meir proved a skillful negotiator whose humor and nonthreatening personal style concealed an immensely tough inner core. Steadfastly refusing to withdraw from the

disputed territories that Israel had invaded and occupied in 1967, Meir met her downfall in 1973, when Egyptian and Syrian troops attacked Israel on Yom Kippur, Judaism's highest holy day. Israeli troops were caught unaware and managed to repel the attack only at the cost of heavy casualties. Battered by criticism for being unprepared, Meir resigned a year later, saying, "I have had enough." Yet to modern Israelis, she remains one of the country's great leaders, a beloved mother among the founding fathers.

[*Golda Meir with Israel's first Prime Minister, David Ben-Gurion. He once called her "the only man in the cabinet." Known as a tough military leader, Meir (right) inspects an honor guard.*]

66

A leader who
doesn't hesitate
before he
sends his nation
into battle
is not fit to be
a leader.

99

RIGOBERTA MENCHÚ CAME OF AGE DURING GUATEMALA'S 33-YEAR CIVIL WAR, ONE OF THE CENTURY'S LONGEST-RUNNING CONFLICTS, AND WENT ON TO BECOME THE CONSCIENCE OF AN ENTIRE CONTINENT. BY SPEAKING out on behalf of the indigenous peoples of Latin America, she has brought hope to thousands who previously had almost none. ¶ A Quiché Maya Indian, Menchú grew up amid the dire poverty enforced by Guatemala's systematic racial discrimination. As a child she saw two brothers die and her father, a well-known peasants' labor organizer, get arrested repeatedly. In 1981, Menchú fled Guatemala after losing three more family members: Her father was incinerated when government troops burned down the Spanish embassy in which he and 38 other union organizers had taken refuge; her mother was raped, then tortured to death by government soldiers; a third brother was burned at the stake as a "subversive." ¶ Menchú told her harrowing story in *I, Rigoberta Menchú*, her 1983 autobiography. But even as she was gaining the world's ear, the situation in her country took a turn for the worse. Pressed by growing insurgency, the military-controlled government annihilated several hundred Indian villages. Some 50,000 people died, pushing the total dead in the long war toward 150,000. Thousands more became refugees. ¶ Branded an enemy of the state, Menchú traveled the world publicizing the plight of the oppressed Mayan population. In recognition, the Nobel committee awarded her the 1992 peace prize, calling her "a vivid symbol of peace and reconciliation across ethnic, cultural, and social dividing lines." ¶ Menchú used her award to set up a Mexico-based human rights foundation for native peoples throughout North and South America. In 1993, she returned to Guatemala, where government and rebel leaders had finally begun peace talks. The challenge now, Menchú said, as the factions signed a historic peace accord, was to build a new society in which *all* citizens were respected.

> **"**
> The only thing
> I wish for is
> freedom for
> Indians wherever
> they are.
> **"**

r i g o b e r t a
Menchú

sandra day O'Connor

1930—

IN 1981, SANDRA DAY O'CONNOR BECAME THE FIRST WOMAN TO GAIN ADMITTANCE INTO THE MOST EXCLUSIVE ALL-MEN'S CLUB IN THE WORLD: THE UNITED STATES SUPREME Court. As such, O'Connor defies easy characterization. When President Ronald Reagan, seeking to fulfill a campaign promise to name a woman to the first available Court opening, tapped her for the job, she was an Arizona state appeals judge and former Republican state legislator who had never served in the federal judiciary at any level. Liberal critics worried that she would end up in thrall to her more experienced conservative colleagues. Conservatives complained that O'Connor's record on abortion did not conform sufficiently to pro-life dogma. O'Connor went on to confound both camps. ¶ A deliberate, cautious, and independent jurist, she more than any other justice has sought middle ground on an ideologically divided court, often casting decisive votes on the day's critical issues, such as abortion, affirmative action, and separation of church and state. By 1993, after a dozen years on the Court, O'Connor had become in the opinion of the American Bar Association "arguably the most influential woman official in the United States." ¶ Graduating third in her Stanford law school class of 1952 (future Supreme Court colleague William Rehnquist was valedictorian), she was turned down for an associate's position by every top law firm in California. A lone Los Angeles firm offered her employment—as a legal secretary. Had it not been for the women's movement, O'Connor acknowledged a year after her appointment to the Supreme Court, "I would not be serving in this job." It is a job this wife and mother of three grown sons clearly relishes. Moderating between the Court's liberal and conservative blocs, the resolutely independent O'Connor has established herself as an all-important swing voter. As she goes, so goes, quite often, the Court—and with it the country.

> **The important fact about my appointment is not that I will decide cases as a woman, but that I am a woman who will get to decide cases.**

> "If you bungle raising your kids, I don't think whatever else you do well matters very much."

1929—1994 IN A COUNTRY WITHOUT ROYALTY, JACQUELINE BOUVIER KENNEDY ONASSIS BECAME ROYAL BY POPULAR ACCLAMATION. FROM THE TIME SHE WAS NAMED "QUEEN DEB OF THE YEAR" AT HER 1947 COMING-OUT PARTY IN NEWPORT, RHODE ISLAND, UNTIL HER DEATH in 1994, beautiful, charming, inscrutable Jackie lived like a sovereign in the public eye. Yet despite being one of the most written-about and photographed women on earth, she remained somehow aloof, a silent enigma marked by tragedy. ¶ Jacqueline Bouvier married the dashing junior senator from Massachusetts in 1953. John Kennedy already had his eye on the presidency and his new wife's vibrancy nicely complemented his ambition. Eight years later, as a stylish young mother of 31, Jackie Kennedy brought unparalleled panache to the role of First Lady. She directed a major restoration of the White House and sparked in the nation's capital a new interest in culture. But it was her beauty and her elegant, understated style that truly enthralled America. Women everywhere emulated her sporty bouffant hairstyle and shaped suits with matching pillbox hats. Even JFK occasionally played second fiddle to his captivating wife, joking on one diplomatic trip about being "the man who accompanied Jacqueline Kennedy to Paris." Publicly at least (his infidelities went unreported until after his death), they were a dream couple. ¶ The dream ended on November 22, 1963, in Dallas, Jackie unforgettably cradling her slain husband's head in her lap as their car sped toward Parkland Memorial Hospital. As a 34-year-old widow, she rose to the task of planning every detail of the dramatic state funeral that was held three days later in Washington. ¶ Her unlikely 1968 marriage to Greek shipping tycoon Aristotle Onassis shocked many Americans. After his death seven years later, she won a $26 million settlement from his estate. Getting on with her life, Onassis threw herself into motherhood (her two children, Caroline and John, Jr., developed into remarkably well-adjusted and productive adults) and began work as a book editor in New York. And she settled into a long, companionable relationship with financier Maurice Tempelsman. ¶ Her death from cancer in 1994 became, like so many events in her life, a quasipublic occasion, an opportunity for her subjects to revisit, in print and on film, the familiar iconography: Jackie on the beach with Jack; Jackie with the children at his funeral; Jackie snapped by paparazzi in New York's Central Park. A Sotheby's auction of items from her estate generated unprecedented interest (and sales). It was almost as if her adoring public believed that in death they could finally get close to the queen who remained so elusive and unknowable in life.

jacqueline bouvier

Kennedy Onassis

rosa Parks

1913—

ON DECEMBER 1, 1955, A 42-YEAR-OLD SEAMSTRESS FROM MONTGOMERY, ALABAMA, STARTED A REVOLUTION. ROSA PARKS GOT ON A CITY BUS THAT AFTERNOON, EXHAUSTED FROM A LONG DAY OF SEWING AT A LOCAL DEPARTMENT store, and took an empty seat in the "colored" section. A Montgomery ordinance required that blacks not only be barred from the front of the bus, but that they relinquish their seats in the middle to any white left standing. As the front of the bus filled up, the white driver ordered Parks to give up her seat to a white man. She stayed put. The driver called the police; Parks was arrested on the spot. "I had been pushed as far as I could stand to be pushed," she later wrote. "I had decided that I would have to know once and for all what rights I had as a human being and a citizen." ¶ Parks had long been active in the local NAACP, and after her arrest and release on $100 bail, the city's African-American leaders—who had been waiting for the right moment to challenge the bus law—quickly rallied around her. A bus boycott was planned for December 5, the day of Parks's trial. After she was

People always say I didn't give up my seat because I was tired, but that isn't true. No, the only tired I was, was tired of giving in.

found guilty, the one-day boycott stretched into 381 days, as authorities rejected the protesters' modest demands: courtesy to black riders, the hiring of black drivers, and the right of blacks to remain seated. (The edict that they stay in the back of the bus was not even challenged.) Thousands of demonstrators—virtually all of the city's 48,000 blacks and some white sympathizers—endured firebombings, police harassment, and trials for conspiracy. Inspired by the oratory of the boycott's leader, a local clergyman named Martin Luther King, Jr., they convened in churches and transformed old hymns and spirituals into "freedom songs," which they sang as they trudged back and forth to work. ¶ The standoff ended only when the Supreme Court ruled all bus segregation illegal. One of the most successful nonviolent protests in American history, the Montgomery Bus Boycott transformed King into the spiritual leader of an entire movement and it secured Parks's status as, in *Ebony* magazine's words, the "living black woman who has done the most to advance the cause of civil rights."

> "When you put your hand to the plow, you can't put it down until you get to the end of the row."

alice Paul

1885—1977 EARLY ON IN HER LIFELONG FIGHT FOR EQUALITY, ALICE PAUL NOTED THE INDIFFERENCE THAT MET SUFFRAGISTS' DEMURE REQUESTS AND DEMANDED THAT WOMEN TAKE OFF THEIR KID GLOVES AND GET TOUGH. NOISY PARADES, WHITE HOUSE PICKETS, police confrontations, arrest, incarceration, and hunger strikes: These were the bold, and ultimately successful, tools of a champion political organizer whose street activism continues to serve as a model for popular protest movements. ¶ After graduating from college in 1905, Paul went to England, where she came under the influence of militant British suffragist Emmeline Pankhurst. During her time there, Paul was arrested repeatedly and

imprisoned three times. ¶ Returning to the United States in 1910, Paul put her new militancy to work. In 1913, with huge crowds gathered in Washington for Woodrow Wilson's inauguration, Paul (keenly aware of the value of publicity) staged a protest parade. As 5,000 women marched down Pennsylvania Avenue, unruly mobs of jeering men tried to block their path to the White House. The police stepped in, to no avail. Forty people landed in the hospital, and Army troops had to restore order. Paul could not have orchestrated it better: The antisuffragists had demonstrated their brutality before the world. ¶ Four years later, when Paul led a National Women's Party picket of the White House, she was remanded to the psychiatric unit of a federal prison. She endured brutal conditions until a newspaper exposé turned public opinion in her favor and Wilson pardoned her in 1918. Two months later, Wilson (knowing the vote for women was essential to the U.S. effort in World War I) did an about-face on suffrage. In 1920, the 19th Amendment became law—the high point of Paul's lifetime of activism. ¶ But women's equality depended on more than the vote. Paul became a lawyer, and in 1923 wrote the Equal Rights Amendment. The fiery feminist was still around to exult in 1972 when Congress finally passed the amendment, which was expected to win quick ratification. Paul died in 1977, and thus was spared the sad spectacle of ERA's death in 1982, just three states short of ratification.

FROM THE MOMENT THAT FRANCES PERKINS ARRIVED IN WASHINGTON IN 1933 AS PART OF FRANKLIN D. ROOSEVELT'S NEW DEAL BRAIN trust, the prim, dark-haired Secretary of Labor put every ounce of her formidable energy into weaving a safety net for Depression-scarred Americans. And as the first woman ever to hold a Cabinet post, she did it amid an atmosphere of hostility, criticism, and relentless scrutiny. Serving throughout Roosevelt's 12 years in office (longer than any Cabinet member in history), Perkins helped create some of the century's great landmarks of social reform, including the Social Security Act of 1935 and the 1938 Fair Labor Standards Act, which established two mainstays of modern labor—the 40-hour work week and the minimum wage. ¶ Perkins began her social activism as a volunteer at Jane Addams's Hull House in Chicago. But the pivotal experience of her political life occurred in 1911, when she watched helplessly as 146 women garment workers died in New York City's infamous Triangle Shirtwaist fire, many leaping to their deaths because the sweatshop building lacked fire escapes. "I felt," Perkins said later, "I must sear it not only on my mind but on my heart as a never-to-be-forgotten reminder of why I had to spend my life fighting conditions that could permit such a tragedy." ¶ Beginning in 1918 under Governor Al Smith, then continuing under Governor Franklin Roosevelt, Perkins went on to expose negligent employers as a New York State industrial commissioner. It was her first salaried position, and she needed every penny: Her husband, economist Paul Caldwell Wilson, had suffered a breakdown after bad investments left the couple and their young daughter financially bereft. (He spent the rest of his life in and out of mental institutions.) ¶ After FDR tapped her as Labor Secretary, Perkins quickly earned a reputation as a master deal-maker. In the words of one admiring insider, she was "a half-loaf girl: Take what you can get now, and try for more later." It was a winning strategy: During her record-setting run on the Cabinet and later as a Civil Service commissioner in the Truman administration, Perkins secured more benefits for the American worker than anyone before or since.

> **"**
>
> **I had been taught**
>
> **long ago by my**
>
> **grandmother**
>
> **that if anybody**
>
> **opens a door,**
>
> **one should always**
>
> **go through.**
>
> **"**

f r a n c e s

Perkins

 e v a

Perón

> **I just use money for the poor. I can't stop to count it.**

1919—1952

EVA PERÓN'S ENTIRE POLITICAL CAREER, FROM MARRIAGE TO GRAVE, LASTED ONLY EIGHT YEARS. YET MORE THAN perhaps any other woman of her time, she embodies the 20th-century notion of the cult of personality. Hers is a classic rags-to-riches tale of theatrical proportions (a fact well recognized by Andrew Lloyd Webber, the creator of the musical *Evita*). The illegitimate daughter of a ranch hand in remote Argentina, she fled rural poverty for the bright lights of Buenos Aires, transformed herself into a glamorous radio actress, and met and eventually married ambitious politician Juan Perón, who was smitten by her beauty and personal magnetism. So were the Argentine people. ¶ When Perón, a disciple of Mussolini, was elected president in 1946, Eva became a self-appointed defender of the poor. Darling of the trade unions, outspoken proponent of women's rights, patron of a thousand charities, she soon became South America's most adored woman (by the masses) and its most resented (by the ruling classes). A formidable politician in her own right, she announced her intention to run for vice president in 1951, but the Army blocked her appointment. ¶ Perón's story is also irresistibly tragic: Stricken with uterine cancer, she died at 33 after a short and ravaging illness. Tens of thousands of people took to the streets of Buenos Aires to mourn her. Juan Perón, who had been reelected with her help (during campaign appearances she was sedated and propped against an invisible support), vowed to pay tribute with a towering monument. In Rome, the Vatican was inundated with some 40,000 letters requesting her canonization. ¶ Hardly as saintly as her admirers believed, Evita (as she was popularly known) routinely resorted to Machiavellian stratagems. Much of the money she funneled to her causes (number one of which was stuffing her Swiss bank accounts) had Perónist graft and extortion as its source. She delighted in using government as an instrument of revenge against personal enemies, and her lavish tastes in clothing and jewels were underwritten by the state. ¶ Beyond dispute is her near-religious hold on Argentinians. After Perón was overthrown in 1955, the ruling junta seized Eva's embalmed corpse (an object of public veneration) removed it from public view, and shipped it to Italy. Three years later, when Perón died in Buenos Aires (having resumed the presidency), her body was displayed alongside his, then finally given a proper burial in a family crypt. Legions of admirers still flock to it yearly, bearing flowers.

Jiang Qing

> **Down with revisionism. Revolution is no crime.**

1913—1991

IN A COUNTRY WHERE FEMALES ARE SO LITTLE VALUED THAT PARENTS OFTEN SIMPLY ABANDON INFANT DAUGHTERS, CHINESE REVOLUTIONARY heroine Jiang Qing amassed astonishing personal and political power. Fourth wife of Communist Party Chairman Mao Zedong, Jiang was with Mao at the front when he defeated Nationalist forces in January 1949 and stood by him in Beijing nine months later when he announced the birth of the People's Republic. But Madame Mao—shrewd, ambitious, ruthless—rose to become a feared leader in her own right. As head of the Gang of Four, a cadre of extremists within China's government, she helped orchestrate the 10-year period of murder and mayhem known as the Cultural Revolution. ¶ Jiang had an unlikely background to become the Robespierre of Communist China. In the 1930s, she was a B-movie vamp who fancied herself the Chinese Greta Garbo. But after meeting Mao and being dazzled by his revolutionary fervor, Jiang dedicated herself to purging China of bourgeois influences, beginning with her own appearance: Her seductive silk gowns were replaced with the severe black tunic and horn-rimmed glasses of a Chinese revolutionary. ¶ Jiang attained her greatest influence beginning in 1966 when Mao unleashed the Cultural Revolution to purge the Chinese Communist Party of "enemies." The Red Guards, teenaged radicals recruited from the countryside, were dispatched to disrupt schools, root out capitalists, and execute traitors. An estimated 400,000 people died during the sustained riot of the Cultural Revolution, and a million more were touched by the violence—to the point where even the aging dictator grew disenchanted with his grand experiment. ¶ Jiang was a different story. As leader of the Gang of Four, she encouraged the outrages of the Red Guard. Anyone in the government who stood in her way was liable to be shipped off to a work farm, or worse: One minister was beaten to death. Soon after Mao died in 1976, Jiang and her Gang of Four cronies (all male) were arrested. ¶ Charged with "towering and heinous" crimes, Jiang was the star defendant in an infamous 1980 show trial. Expected (indeed scripted) to admit guilt, the defiant widow remained unrepentant to the end. The outcome was a foregone conclusion: Jiang was convicted and sentenced to death. (Chinese leaders, fearing reprisals from hard-core Maoists, ultimately commuted her sentence to life in prison.) She hanged herself in 1991 while still under house arrest.

Jiang Qing faced numerous charges, including causing the death of 35,000 people during the Cultural Revolution. Her 1980 trial led to a sentence of life in prison.

35

eleanor
Roosevelt

1884—1962

LIONIZED IN HER LIFETIME AS "FIRST LADY TO THE WORLD," ELEANOR ROOSEVELT OVERCAME ACUTE PERSONAL SORROW TO BECOME THE MOST INFLUENTIAL AMERICAN WOMAN OF HER OWN OR ANY OTHER TIME. HUMANITARIAN, SOCIAL WORKER, CIVIL rights activist, Roosevelt felt a deep affinity with the poor and disenfranchised, and fought tirelessly on their behalf. ¶ Having lost both her father, whom she idolized, and her mother, whom she feared, by the age of 10, Roosevelt spent the balance of her childhood in the austere household of her maternal grandmother, feeling emotionally isolated and, as she later wrote, "like a little old woman entirely lacking in the spontaneous joy and mirth of youth." At 15, she was sent to Allenswood, a school in England run by the leftist social reformer Marie Souvestre. There, under Souvestre's care and guidance, Roosevelt blossomed. "Whatever I have become since," she said later, "had its seeds in those three years of contact with a liberal mind and strong personality." Returning to America in 1902, Roosevelt worked with poor immigrants in New York City's settlement houses and became a staunch advocate of workers' rights. ¶ In 1905, she married her fifth cousin Franklin Delano Roosevelt and soon added mother (six children in 10 years) and wife to her growing list of achievements. Although her public devotion to her husband never wavered, she was deeply wounded by the discovery, in 1918, of his affair with her social secretary Lucy Mercer. From that point on, Roosevelt withdrew from her husband and threw her emotional energies into social causes and a vast and eclectic assortment of friends. When polio paralyzed FDR in 1921, his wife became both his nurse and his personal political emissary. ¶ From FDR's election in 1932 until his death in 1945, Roosevelt radically redefined the role of First Lady. Crisscrossing the country to observe firsthand the abysmal

> **"** It is better to light a candle than to curse the darkness. **"**

conditions in urban slums and on failing farms, among blacks in the deep South, and in coal mines, factories, and prisons, she emerged as the public conscience of the New Deal. She also wrote a newspaper column, "My Day," as well as several books, including *This Is My Story*, serialized throughout 1937 in *Ladies' Home Journal*. ¶ After FDR's death, President Truman appointed Roosevelt a delegate to the newly formed United Nations. There, she pursued a long-held dream—the drafting of the Universal Declaration of Human Rights. When it passed the General Assembly in 1948 (an accomplishment many historians consider her finest), the delegates gave her a standing ovation. ¶ Remaining politically engaged throughout the 1950s, Roosevelt stood firmly against McCarthyism, lectured on human rights, and supported the presidential campaigns of her good friend Adlai Stevenson. Her final official appointment was to John F. Kennedy's Commission on the Status of Women, which she chaired until six months before her death.

> **ERA is a cadaver that we have to keep pushing back into the coffin.**

1924— PHYLLIS SCHLAFLY WILL FOREVER BE REMEMBERED AS THE WOMAN WHO SHOT DOWN THE EQUAL RIGHTS AMENDMENT. BUT THE ANTIFEMINIST LEADER MADE HER MARK ON SOCIETY IN OTHER WAYS AS WELL. FOUNDER OF THE ARCHCONSERVATIVE EAGLE Forum, Schlafly led crusades against legal abortion, popular revolution in Latin America, sex on television, and nuclear arms control. The bomb, she once said, is "a marvelous gift that was given to our country by a wise God." A tireless organizer who in her Reagan-era heyday had a finger in many political pies (she even dreamed of being named Secretary of Defense), Schlafly belonged to the great political tradition of resistance: She wielded influence not by engineering change, but by standing resolutely against it. ¶ By the time Schlafly joined the fight against ERA in 1972, she had already run two losing campaigns for Congress and written a handful of conservative-themed books, including *A Choice, Not an Echo* about failed 1964 presidential candidate Barry

Goldwater. An expert spin doctor in an age before the practice had a name, Schlafly fanned popular fears about the amendment. Its passage, she warned, would leave non-working married women without financial means, force public restrooms to become unisex, encourage homosexual marriage, and require women to go into combat. Polls consistently showed that two-thirds of the American people supported ERA, but the amendment died in 1982, just three states short of ratification. "ERA," she exulted, "will take its place with the Prohibition and the child labor amendments as ones which did not have enough support of the American people to be in the Constitution." ¶ A mother of six, Schlafly always maintained the primacy of child-rearing, but she was herself a prototype for "Supermom," juggling career and family from the beginning of her 1949 marriage to John Fred Schlafly, Jr., a politically conservative Illinois lawyer. "But my husband understands," she once said, "I'm a housewife, but not *just* a housewife." For her vanquished opponents in the women's movement, that crucial distinction was a hard-won lesson.

phyllis Schlafly

gloria
Steinem

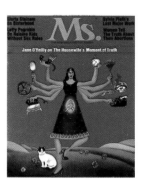

1934—

> **66**
>
> **Some of us**
>
> **are becoming**
>
> **the men**
>
> **we wanted**
>
> **to marry.**
>
> **99**

CHARISMATIC, ARTICULATE, AND DROP-DEAD GORGEOUS, GLORIA STEINEM BECAME IN THE 1970S THE POPULAR EMBODIMENT OF THE BURGEONING WOMEN'S MOVEMENT. THROUGH HER UNSTINTING WORK AS A JOURNALIST, PUBLIC SPEAKER, AND FOUNDING EDITOR OF *Ms.*, the world's first mass-market feminist magazine, Steinem helped break women's liberation out of the ghettos of academia and radical politics and move it into the mainstream of American life. ¶ A 1956 graduate of Smith College, Steinem made a splash as a journalist with a 1963 *Show* magazine article about her experience of going undercover as a "bunny" in a New York City Playboy Club. By 1968, by virtue of her coverage of such events as the explosive Democratic National Convention in Chicago, she was seen as a bright young journalistic star. ¶ Steinem's feminist conversion was clinched when she was covering abortion law hearings in New York in 1968. "I will never forget that night as long as I live, because I heard women stand up and tell the truth in public for the first time in my life," she later wrote. "For me, that was the moment when the light bulb began to come on." She started to write about women's rights with increasing vigor, even going public with the story of the abortion she had endured in utter solitude when she was 22. ¶ A few years later, Steinem and five partners conceived of *Ms.* as a "how-to" magazine—"not how to make jelly," Steinem wrote, "but how to seize control of your life." The premier issue hit the newsstands in 1972; within a year, *Ms.* had an estimated 1.4 million readers. ¶ Steinem's brand of optimistic pragmatism was sometimes criticized as "too soft" by radical factions within the movement (and there is no question that her glamorous good looks and staunch heterosexuality helped make feminism more palatable to the masses). But through it all Steinem has been first and foremost a humanist who believes that the liberation of women will, in the end, liberate men as well.

daw aung san **SuuKyi**

1945— HUMAN RIGHTS ACTIVIST DAW AUNG SAN SUU KYI IS THE POLITICAL CONSCIENCE OF A NATION. ON HER SLENDER SHOULDERS SQUARELY REST THE DEMOCRATIC DREAMS OF THE MILLIONS of Burmese people living under one of Asia's most repressive military regimes. Suu Kyi has paid a dear price for accepting this burden: detention, enforced separation from her husband and sons, physical abuse, even the threat of death. Through this ordeal, she has remained upbeat, caustically funny, and unremittingly brave. "You know how it is with these dictatorial governments," she said with a shrug after being freed from six years of house arrest in 1995. "If you're part of the movement for democracy in Burma, imprisonment is simply an occupational hazard." ¶ For years, politics did not intrude on the life Suu Kyi had made in England with her husband, Michael Aris, a Tibetan scholar at Oxford University, and their two sons. She had not lived in Burma since 1960, yet the country remained close to her heart: Her father, U Aung San, had led Burma's fight for independence from Great Britain after World War II, only to be assassinated by a right-wing political group in 1947, just months before independence was formally achieved. ¶ In mid-1988, Suu Kyi's

mother suffered a stroke. With a sense of foreboding, she returned at long last to her homeland. Her visit coincided with a spontaneous popular uprising against the country's quarter-century-old dictatorship. The army was sent out, and within days, 3,000 unarmed protesters had been gunned down. "As my father's daughter," said Suu Kyi, "I felt I had a duty to get involved." Some 500,000 antigovernment protesters gathered at the country's most sacred shrine in Rangoon to hear Suu Kyi speak. She told the crowd that they had a fundamental human right to choose their own government, and, overnight, what had been an unfocused outpouring of antigovernment passion became a bona fide democratic movement. ¶ Suu Kyi went on to help found the National League for Democracy (NLD), which in the months ahead became the leading opposition party in Myanmar (as Burma was named under the junta). Placed under armed guard in her own house, she was given a simple choice: Leave the country at once, or remain under arrest indefinitely. She chose to stay. Three years would pass before the government so much as allowed her husband to visit. By then Suu Kyi had become one of the world's most famous dissidents, winning the 1991 Nobel Peace Prize for her use of "nonviolent means to resist a regime characterized by brutality." Suu Kyi remained in detention for six full years. When she was finally allowed to walk free in 1995, one of her first acts was to lay a bouquet of flowers on her father's grave. To this day, Suu Kyi continues the fight that claimed her father more than 50 years ago.

> **"**
>
> It's not bravery.
>
> It's a question
>
> of doing what you
>
> have to do.
>
> You can go ahead
>
> with what you're
>
> doing or you
>
> can run away.
>
> **"**

> "
>
> Each of us
>
> is merely a
>
> small instrument;
>
> all of us, after
>
> accomplishing
>
> our mission,
>
> will disappear.
>
> "

Mother Teresa

1910—1997 IN AN AGE MORE NOTABLE FOR CYNICISM AND GREED THAN FOR COMPASSION AND CHARITY, THE ROMAN CATHOLIC NUN KNOWN SIMPLY AS MOTHER TERESA INSPIRED MILLIONS WITH HER ABSOLUTE DEVOTION TO THE WORLD'S DISPOSSESSED. UP UNTIL HER death in 1997, this diminutive woman ministered to the poorest of the poor, the sickest of the sick. Through it all, her single, unchanging mission was to bring dignity and relief to those whom society has discarded. To her legions of admirers, she was a living saint. ¶ Agnes Gonxha Bojaxhiu was born in Albania in 1910, the daughter of a prosperous construction contractor. At 17, the girl her brother Lazar remembered as "a real tomboy—plump, fun-loving, and mischievous" entered the Sisters of Loreto order. "Do you realize you are burying yourself?" her brother asked. "How could a girl like you become a nun?" ¶ Assigned to St. Mary's High School in Calcutta, Sister Teresa, as she was now known (after Saint Therese, the patron saint of missionaries), spent nearly two decades teaching geography to mostly middle-class girls—a job she came to believe provided insufficient service both to God and to her fellow man. She had become increasingly distressed by the horrific living conditions that festered on Calcutta's streets and was even more affected by a bloody riot between Hindus and Muslims that she witnessed in 1946, as India was caught up in its drive toward independence. ¶ Heeding what she would later describe as "the call within a call," Sister Teresa decided, as she put it, "to leave the convent and help the poor while living among them." It

was, she said, a command from God. In 1950, she founded the Order of the Missionaries of Charity, dedicated to the alleviation of human suffering. Her mission attracted several followers, who adopted as their uniform the now-familiar blue-banded white cotton habit. Today, the order has thousands of members in some 90 countries and operates more than 500 homes and clinics. ¶ Possessed of a belief in the preciousness and dignity of human life that was as unshakable as her deep religious faith, Mother Teresa received countless honors, but always discounted her own importance. "I am nothing," she would say. "God is all." In 1979 she was awarded the Nobel Peace Prize. "The loneliest, the most wretched and the dying," said the Nobel Committee, "have at her hands received compassion without condescension, based on reverence for man." Mother Teresa responded with typical humility. "Personally, I am unworthy," she said. "I accept in the name of the poor."

1925 —

UPON BECOMING PRIME MINISTER OF GREAT BRITAIN IN 1979, MARGARET THATCHER SET THREE BASIC GOALS FOR HER CONSERVATIVE GOVERNMENT: TO HALT HER COUNTRY'S uninterrupted postwar economic slide, curb the power of trade unions, and root out the socialism that she believed was weakening what had once been the world's greatest power. Over the next 11 years—the longest term of any 20th-century British leader, including Winston Churchill—the so-called "Thatcher Revolution" changed the way Britain did business. ¶ The daughter of a provincial grocer who attended Oxford on scholarship, Thatcher came to the Conservative Party from outside traditional ruling-class channels. After being elected to the House of Commons in 1959, she rose quickly within the party ranks, becoming a minister for education and science in 1970 and getting elected as leader of the Conservatives in 1975. Four years later, with a general strike hobbling the country, Thatcher and the Conservatives were swept into power on a wave of popular discontent. She thus became the first woman to head a major Western democracy. ¶ Putting to rest any doubts that a woman could govern as forcefully as a man, the new prime minister pursued her goals with a single-minded intensity that earned her the sobriquet "Iron Lady." She slashed taxes and dismantled the welfare state, "privatizing" hundreds of industries. She stood fast in her belief that Northern Ireland should remain part of the United Kingdom (surviving an assassination attempt by the IRA in the bargain) and in her opposition to a borderless European Community with a single currency. In 1982, she waged war against Argentina over the last vestiges of Empire in the Falkland Islands. Her supply-side economic policies were alternately lauded for helping create a profit-driven free-enterprise system, and reviled for creating a yawning economic gap between England's haves and have-nots. Indeed, it was her perceived indifference to the poor, in the form of a newly implemented "poll tax" (a stiff local levy imposed on every adult), that led to her ouster in 1990. ¶ Yet, despite its architect's departure from center stage, Thatcherism remains a potent force in Great Britain. Even under a Labour government, the country is unlikely to deviate from the free-market course she steered.

margaret

Thatcher

I have a
woman's ability
to stick to a job
and get on with it
when everyone
else walks off
and leaves.

"

Writers & Journa

lists

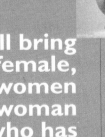

"A woman writer will bring certain gear with her, having been born female, having been born into, maybe, a society where women are not valued very much. But a woman writer tells us that here comes somebody who has decided she's come to stay."

—Maya Angelou

m a y a

Angelou

1928—

A "PEOPLE'S POET RATHER THAN A POET'S POET," AS ONE COMMENTATOR PUTS IT, MAYA ANGELOU HAS BEEN A NIGHTCLUB SINGER, AN ESSAYIST, A SCREENWRITER, A MADAM, A COLLEGE PROFESSOR, A DANCER, A NEWSPAPER JOURNALIST, A Broadway actress, a streetcar conductor, and a political activist. In *I Know Why the Caged Bird Sings*, her searing 1970 account of growing up poor and black during the Depression, Angelou pioneered the use of fictional techniques in autobiography and helped establish the memoir as a popular literary genre. Even more resonant with Angelou's vast public was *On the Pulse of Morning*, the inspirational poem she delivered at President Clinton's 1993 inauguration. With it, she became, by popular acclamation, the nation's first poet. ¶ Born Marguerite Johnson in St. Louis, Angelou had a tumultuous childhood marked by parental desertion when she was 3 years old ("Our parents had decided to put an end to their calamitous marriage," she writes matter-of-factly in *I Know Why the Caged Bird Sings*, "and Father shipped us home to his mother") and rape (by her mother's boyfriend) when she was 8. The latter was especially traumatic, and when her assailant was found beaten to death—possibly by Angelou's incensed uncles—the girl was so overcome with shame and guilt that she stopped speaking for several years. During this silent period, spent largely in Stamps, Arkansas, she discovered literature, immersing herself in the works of Shakespeare, Poe, and Dickens, as well as such leading African-American literary figures as Paul Lawrence Dunbar, James Weldon Johnson, and Langston Hughes. ¶ The author of several volumes of poetry and a total of six autobiographical books, including *All God's Children Need Traveling Shoes* (1986) and *Wouldn't Take Nothing for My Journey Now* (1993), Angelou also was the first black woman to write a screenplay that was made into a film, *Georgia, Georgia,* in 1972. Two decades later, her recitation at Clinton's swearing-in ceremony marked the first time a poet had participated in an inauguration since Robert Frost read at John F. Kennedy's in 1961.

1906-1975

A GERMAN JEW WHO FLED TO FRANCE BEFORE WORLD WAR II THEN ESCAPED OCCUPIED FRANCE TO THE UNITED STATES, HANNAH ARENDT WROTE FROM A UNIQUELY PERSONAL PERSPECTIVE WHEN SHE CITED the Holocaust as the supreme example of "the banality of evil." That phrase, from her 1963 book *Eichmann in Jerusalem*, is one of the most penetrating in modern political thought. And Arendt was one of the century's most insightful thinkers, writing half a dozen books that together form a cornerstone of contemporary political philosophy. ¶ Raised in what was then East Prussia, Arendt arrived in the United States from France in 1941. In New York, her political and literary essays soon attracted the attention of the city's intellectual elite. Larger fame came in 1951, with the publication of *The Origins of Totalitarianism,* which traces both fascism and communism to 19th-century imperialism and bourgeois anti-Semitism. ¶ In her most controversial work, *Eichmann in Jerusalem,* Arendt wrote that to single out Eichmann for Holocaust guilt was both irresponsible and histrionic: It endowed him with powers he did not have. Eichmann, she said, was just one of many individually ordinary human cogs—German, non-German, even Jewish—whose active or passive assent allowed the Holocaust to happen. Far from a devil incarnate, Eichmann was "terribly and terrifyingly normal." (Hence, his "banality.") ¶ Arendt's analysis, with its hint of self-blame, offended many within the Jewish community. So did the posthumous revelation that, beginning in 1950 and continuing until her death, she had resumed her youthful love affair with the German existentialist Martin Heidegger. A giant of 20th-century philosophy, Heidegger had disgraced himself in the 1930s by publicly joining the Nazi Party and, after the war, refusing to repudiate his actions. That Arendt, the great antitotalitarian philosopher, could overlook this monumental offense galled many observers. But there is perhaps another way to view the matter—as one more expression of the intellectual and emotional freedom that she embodied.

> It is in fact
>
> far easier to act
>
> under conditions
>
> of tyranny than
>
> it is to think.

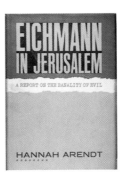

EICHMANN IN JERUSALEM

A REPORT ON THE BANALITY OF EVIL

HANNAH ARENDT

h a n n a h **Arendt**

1907—1964 "A FEW THOUSAND WORDS FROM HER," AN EDITORIALIST ONCE SAID OF RACHEL CARSON, "AND THE WORLD TOOK A NEW DIRECTION." WRITER, SCIENTIST, conservationist, Carson can be credited with founding the modern environmental movement. Before she published *Silent Spring* in 1962, two beliefs held sway: that environmental hazards had been largely eliminated with the end of diseases like smallpox, and that technological progress was a greater good than the natural world it necessarily destroyed. *Silent Spring*, a damning study of the deadly effects of indiscriminate chemical pesticides on fish, bird, and human populations, changed forever those complacent assumptions. ¶ An unlikely crusader, Carson had been content in her dual roles as a government marine biologist and popular science writer. Her trilogy of books about the ocean, *Under the Sea-Wind* (1941), the best-selling *The Sea Around Us* (1951), and *The Edge of the Sea* (1955), had explained marine science to lay readers in clear, poetic prose. But as the evidence against DDT mounted in the 1950s, Carson was impelled by conscience to put aside marine biology and speak out against industrial irresponsibility. "There would be no peace for me," she said, "if I kept silent." ¶ As she began researching *Silent Spring*—a magazine article that quickly grew into a book—her mission took on an almost religious intensity. Carefully and articulately, Carson built her case against government's and industry's wanton poisoning of earth, land, and sea. Never did she argue for a total ban on chemical agents (except indiscriminately lethal compounds, such as DDT), only that they be used with extraordinary caution; and only after their systemic effects had been studied and fully understood. ¶ As Carson had anticipated, the chemical and agricultural industries responded to *Silent Spring* by mounting an ugly smear campaign against her, calling her everything from overly emotional (reading the book, wrote one doctor, was like "arguing with a woman") to unprofessional to a communist. Gravely ill with bone cancer and weighed down with family responsibilities (after her father and a sister died, the unmarried Carson supported her mother, her nieces, and a grand-nephew), she persevered with extraordinary dignity and courage, defending her research, gaining converts, even testifying before a federal scientific advisory committee that President Kennedy created to examine her findings. (The committee's report ended up endorsing them.) Carson died in 1964 at the age of 56—eight years before the U.S. government finally came around to her way of thinking and banned DDT.

rachel
Carson

"

I believe

that whenever we

destroy beauty,

or substitute

something

man-made and

artificial for a

natural feature

of the earth,

we have retarded

some part

of man's

spiritual growth.

"

agatha **Christie**

> **"**
>
> An archaeologist
>
> is the best
>
> husband a
>
> woman can have;
>
> the older she gets
>
> the more
>
> interested he is
>
> in her.
>
> **"**

1890–1976

EVERY SO OFTEN A WRITER CREATES A CHARACTER SO VIBRANT THAT IT ACHIEVES A SORT OF EXTRA-LITERARY IMMORTALITY. FEW AUTHORS CAN PULL OFF THIS TRICK EVEN ONCE. THE BRITISH mystery writer Agatha Christie did it twice. In the fastidious Belgian inspector Hercule Poirot and the eccentric elderly spinster Miss Jane Marple, she invented two of the most familiar and beloved figures in 20th-century fiction. While she was at it, she managed to redeem the lowly murder novel. In her hands, the genre became both respectable and somehow comforting. ¶ Success did not come instantly to Christie. Her first novel, *The Mysterious Affair at Styles,* was rejected by six different publishers. When it finally did make it into print, in 1920, it attracted few readers. Her breakthrough came in 1926 with *The Murder of Roger Ackroyd*. Considered by many aficionados to be the best murder mystery ever written, *Ackroyd* features crisp dialogue, economical description, and the sort of devilishly intricate plot that became Christie's signature. ¶ If *Ackroyd* made Christie famous, subsequent novels— some 60 in all, plus stories, plays, movie scripts, and six more novels written under the pseudonym Mary Westmacott—made her rich. Among English-language writers, only Shakespeare tops her on the all-time sales list. Her 1952 play, *The Mousetrap,* has earned a fortune by itself, running for more than 40 years in London's West End. ¶ A matronly model of British upper-middle-class rectitude, Christie generally led a life as free of suspense as her books were full of it. But on one occasion early in her career, her life did momentarily seem to converge with her art. Just before the publication of *The Murder of Roger Ackroyd*, she disappeared. Her car was found abandoned not far from the home she shared with her husband, a dashing, much-decorated World War I flier who happened to be involved with another woman. Police combed nearby woods and fields, and dredged rivers. When no body was found, the disappearance made its way into the papers, and a national search was launched. Authorities were starting to suspect Archie Christie of murder, when his wife turned up in a hotel in northern England, confused and unable to remember how she had gotten there. ¶ Christie soon recovered from the apparent bout of amnesia (and divorced Archie and later married archaeologist Sir Max Mallowan), but the mystery of her disappearance was never fully resolved. It was the sort of loose end that she would never have allowed into one of her books.

Onscreen, British actress Margaret Rutherford(top,right) brings the character of Miss Marple to life. The full cast gathers (right) to hear the "solution" in And Then There Were None.

de Beauvoir

1908—1986

AT THE CENTER OF SIMONE DE BEAUVOIR'S LIFE AND WORK LIES A DISCOMFITING PARADOX: THE PHILOSOPHER WHO IN HER 1949 MASTERWORK, *THE SECOND SEX*, SO BRILLIANTLY DISSECTED MALE CULTURE'S MARGINALIZATION OF WOMEN WAS HERSELF DEEPLY INFLUENCED, personally and professionally, by a man. That the man, Jean-Paul Sartre, was one of the towering figures of 20th-century intellectual history—and that the couple's long, public, and unconventional partnership was a uniquely balanced one—goes a long way toward explaining the seeming contradiction. ¶ The gifted daughter of a middle-class Parisian family, de Beauvoir at 19 rejected her bourgeois background with a declaration of personal independence: "I don't want my life to obey any other will but my own." At the Sorbonne she studied philosophy and finished second overall in her comprehensive exams—one place behind Sartre. By that time, 1929, the pair had already begun an "open relationship"—one in which they maintained separate apartments and took occasional secondary lovers but otherwise shared everything. (She described him in her autobiography as "a soulmate in whom I found, heated to the point of incandescence, all of my passions.") The relationship endured for a total of 51 years, ending only with Sartre's death in 1980. ¶ A witty and lucid writer, de Beauvoir wrote several acclaimed novels before publishing, in 1949, the epochal work that turned her into an international literary star. An encyclopedic survey of womanhood, *Le Deuxième Sexe*—which was translated and published in the United States in 1953 as *The Second Sex*—is credited with starting the postwar women's movement. ¶ Throughout history, de Beauvoir argued, women from birth have been conditioned to believe in the superiority of men. As "objects" that exist solely for men's pleasure, women are left with "no past, no history, no religion of their own." In the book's most-quoted passage, she wrote, "One is not born, but rather becomes, a woman." ¶ De Beauvoir's daring relationship with Sartre, as well as the iconoclastic nature of her work, made her the sort of radical-chic intellectual celebrity that France has a long tradition of nurturing. The couple edited small journals, championed workers' rights, demonstrated for abortion-law reform, and generally embodied modern ideals of social liberty. ¶ In addition to her own prose, de Beauvoir helped edit Sartre's philosophical works. Her influence is most felt today through *The Second Sex*. De Beauvoir, said Betty Friedan, feminist author who would follow her in writing about both women's subjugation and aging, was "an authentic heroine in the history of womanhood."

> **"**
>
> When we abolish
> the slavery of
> half of humanity,
> together with
> the whole system
> of hypocrisy
> that it implies,
> then the 'division'
> of humanity will
> reveal its genuine
> significance and
> the human couple
> will find
> its true form.
>
> **"**

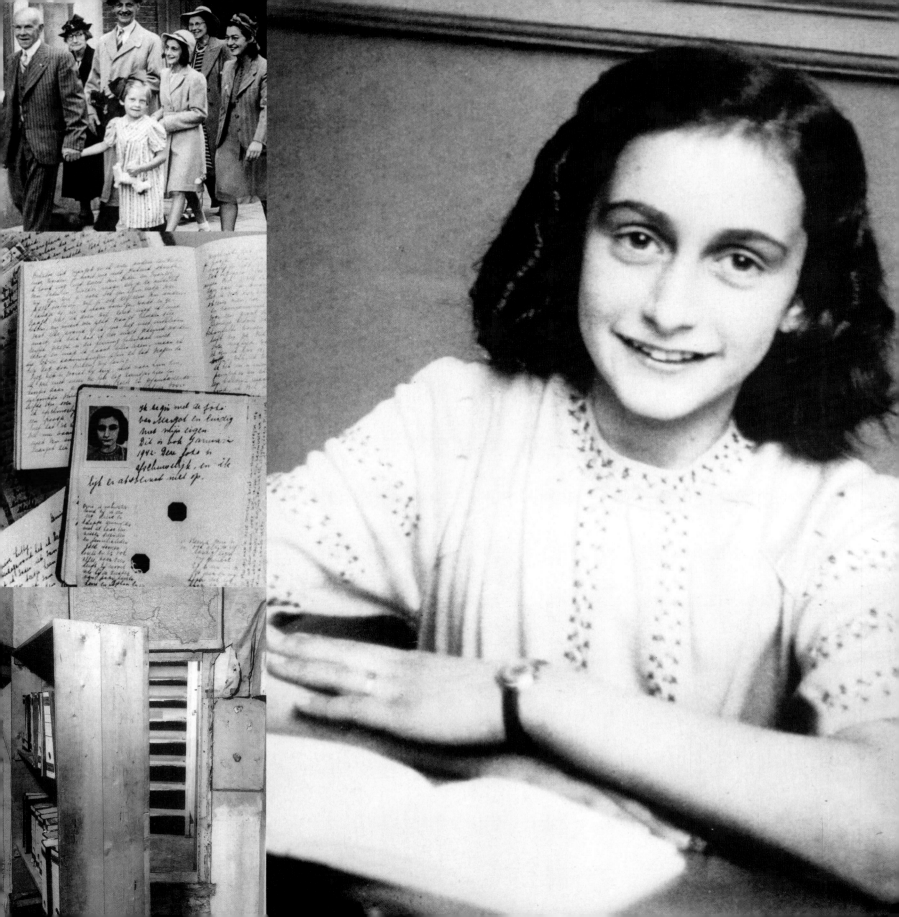

> " In spite of everything, I still believe that people are really good at heart. "

anne Frank

1929—1945 "NO ONE WILL BE INTERESTED IN THE UNBOSOMINGS OF A 13-YEAR-OLD SCHOOLGIRL." SO WROTE THE GERMAN-JEWISH TEENAGER ANNE FRANK IN ONE OF THE NOTEBOOKS SHE WOULD FILL DURING THE TWO YEARS SHE AND HER family spent in hiding in Nazi-occupied Amsterdam. Anything but uninteresting, Anne Frank's diary stands as perhaps the single most poignant human document of history's most inhuman event, the Holocaust. ¶ From June 12, 1942, her 13th birthday, until August 4, 1944, when the Franks were betrayed by a Dutch collaborator and sent to the death camp at Auschwitz, Anne recorded her innermost thoughts and musings on life, puberty, and family. Over every word—written with an honesty, fluency, and freshness of insight that would be impressive in a mature writer and are astonishing in an adolescent—the Gestapo threat hangs ominously. Yet a tender and touching optimism pervades the young writer's pages. The fact that her ultimate fate was such a repudiation of her optimism makes reading her story at times almost unbearably painful. ¶ Born in 1929, Annelies Marie Frank was the second daughter of Otto and Edith Frank, middle-class Jews from Frankfurt, Germany. When Anne was four, the Franks fled the Nazis to Amsterdam. Seven years later, Germany invaded the Netherlands and Otto, who ran a business selling pectin and spices to Dutch women, immediately made plans to hide his family in the attic annex of a warehouse he leased in Amsterdam's narrow old quarter. ¶ The Franks and four associates survived undetected with the help of some of Otto Frank's employees until an informer, most likely a warehouse clerk, tipped off the Nazis. Anne and the others were sent to Auschwitz. She and her sister ultimately died of typhus and starvation in Bergen-Belsen, another camp, in 1945. Of the eight, only Otto Frank survived. ¶ After the war Otto Frank returned to Amsterdam, where he received the diaries that had been courageously retrieved from the annex by Miep Gies, one of the family's protectors. In 1953, the notebooks were released in the United States as *The Diary of a Young Girl.* Since translated into more than 30 languages—and expanded with additional entries (about her mother or her budding sexuality) that her father originally deleted—Anne Frank's adolescent "unbosomings" are an extraordinary testament to humankind's dual capacities for bottomless inhumanity and irrepressible hope in the face of such brutality.

Anne Frank enjoys happier times with her father Otto (top, left). He hid his family well (entrance to their secret shelter is bottom left), but they were discovered and arrested.

Dit is een foto, zoals ik me zou wensen, altijd zo te zijn. Dan had ik nog wel een kans om naar Hollywood te komen.
Anne Frank
10 Oct. 1942

(translation)
"This is a photo as I would wish myself to look all the time. Then I would maybe have a chance to come to Hollywood."
Anne Frank, 10 Oct. 1942

"

The time
is at hand when
the voices
of the feminine
mystique
can no longer
drown out the
inner voice
that is driving
women on
to become
complete.

"

betty Friedan

1921—

THE MODERN WOMEN'S MOVEMENT WAS BORN IN 1963, WHEN BETTY FRIEDAN, A MARRIED MOTHER OF THREE FROM SUBURBAN NEW YORK, PUBLISHED *THE FEMININE MYSTIQUE*. WRITING from the perspective of an educated, comfortable, and profoundly dissatisfied housewife, Friedan offered an angry analysis of sex roles in prosperous postwar America. Suburbia, Friedan alleged, was "a bedroom and kitchen sexual ghetto" and "fulfillment had only one definition for American women after 1949—the housewife-mother." For millions of female readers, the book struck a deep chord,

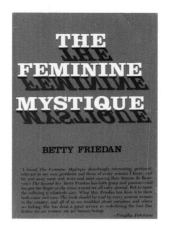

ripping away the facade of their lives and providing them with new ways of seeing and defining themselves. From that moment on, feminism (which had lain dormant in the years following World War II) was launched on its second wave. And this time, as Friedan would later note approvingly, that wave included legions of "conventional" women who had married and borne children. ¶ Graduating at the top of both her high school class in Peoria, Illinois, and her 1942 class at Smith College, Betty Goldstein won research fellowships in psychology (Freud was a particular interest) at the University of California at Berkeley, but eventually opted for a career in journalism. She married Carl Friedan in 1947 and had two children. After having her second child, in the 1950s, she lost a newspaper job because her employer would not grant her a maternity leave. Friedan settled into the role of suburban wife and mother, but instead of the fulfillment she expected, she felt a creeping dissatisfaction. Curious to know if others shared her disenchantment, she polled 200 Smith classmates and discovered that she was not alone. It was then that she began her groundbreaking book. ¶ Assuring women that they were not neurotic for feeling frustrated, she prescribed education and stimulating jobs outside the home. *The Feminine Mystique* became an instant best-seller, and Friedan the leading spokeswoman for a previously voiceless generation of women. She went on to co-found the National Organization for Women (NOW) in 1966, serving as president until 1970. "Women heard about the book," she recalled years later, "and they had this great relief, you know. They stopped me and said, 'Oh, it changed my life. It changed my whole life.'" ¶ In 1993, still dauntless at 71, Friedan wrote *The Fountain of Age*, an attempt to do for elderly Americans what *The Feminine Mystique* had done earlier for women—namely, liberate them from the stifling oppressiveness of stereotypes.

ann Landers

1918— ON THE OCCASION OF HER 40TH ANNIVERSARY AS THE WORLD'S LEADING ADVICE COLUMNIST, ANN LANDERS TOLD AN INTERVIEWER THAT SHE WOULD NEVER RETIRE. "I PLAN TO DIE AT THE TYPEWRITER," she said. The quip touched upon a serious question: Where will 90 million readers of 1,200 newspapers turn for guidance when Landers—tolerant, traditional, and forgiving—finally stops dispensing her homespun wisdom? ¶ Eppie Lederer wrote her first Ann Landers column for the *Chicago Sun-Times* in 1955. The original Ann Landers, a nurse, had died suddenly and the editors wanted to keep the promising new column going. A financially comfortable housewife (her husband Jules was the founder of Budget-Rent-A-Car) and Democratic Party fundraiser who had never held a paying job, Lederer applied for the position along with about 30 other women. In responding to sample questions, she solicited the opinions of various friends she had made in political circles—like Supreme Court Justice William O. Douglas. A few days later, the job was hers. ¶ Having friends in high places may have helped Lederer get the column, but keeping it was her own doing. Day after day she doled out sensible opinions on all manner of personal problems. In the process she became one of the most powerful women in the country. (Landers's identical twin, Abigail Van Buren, followed her minutes-older sister into the advice business, writing a column from San Francisco under the name "Dear Abby.") In Landers's very first year she answered a letter from a young homosexual who was wondering how to break the news to his parents. (She suggested family counseling, revealing a faith in professional expertise that would become one of her trademarks.) The topic spooked publishers, but with Lederer already commanding a large loyal audience they couldn't afford to pull her column. In just this way, straight-shooting ("Wake up and smell the coffee" was a favorite injunction), middle-of-the-road Ann Landers opened conversation on countless social issues.

> **Expect trouble as an inevitable part of your life and repeat to yourself the most comforting words of all: This, too, shall pass.**

1901—1978

MARGARET MEAD'S STATURE RESTS ON TWO IMMENSE CONTRIBUTIONS: SHE OPENED ANTHROPOLOGY TO A popular audience, thereby giving laymen a new tool for understanding their place in the world. And she demonstrated that gender roles are largely determined by culture. In other words, men and women behave in "sex-typed" ways because society expects them to—not because of some universal natural law. ¶ Mead was still a graduate student when, at 24, she embarked on two years of fieldwork on the Polynesian island of Samoa. Up to then, anthropology had been mostly a matter of men studying men, or men studying artifacts. Mead's 1928 book *Coming of Age in Samoa* focused on the island's young women, contrasting their adolescence (a carefree period characterized by uninhibited sexual experimentation) with that of Western girls (frequently traumatic and stress-ridden). Mead famously concluded that culture influences behavior and personality more than do biological factors—specifically sex or race. Revolutionary when it appeared, *Coming of Age* remains the most widely read anthropological study of all time. ¶ A free-spirited gadfly who over the course of her career published two dozen books and a thousand articles, Mead was a lightning rod for controversy. Some scientists—not a few of whom envied her fame and ability to market books—claimed her data collection was selective and her conclusions oversimplified. Conservatives dismissed her as a sexual adventurer too ready to identify with her permissive Oceanic subjects. ¶ Indeed, Mead led a determinedly unconventional life. She married three times, and took lovers of both sexes. When she gave birth in 1939 to her daughter, Mary Catherine Bateson, she insisted on having no anesthesia (then all but universal) because women in the societies she studied never complained of pain during childbirth. Both professionally and personally, Mead was driven, as she wrote in her autobiography, *Blackberry Winter*, by the need "to strip off the layer of culturally attributed expected behavior." ¶ Using the bully pulpit of fame, Mead spoke out on social issues ranging from women's rights, sexual morality, and race relations to conservation and world hunger. Always she came down on the side of compassion, believing that anthropology's ultimate goal was to improve humankind's lot.

> **"**
>
> If we are
>
> to achieve a
>
> richer culture—
>
> one rich
>
> in contrasting
>
> values—
>
> we must
>
> recognize the
>
> whole gamut
>
> of human
>
> potentialities...
>
> **"**

margaret **Mead**

1900—1949

WITH HER FIRST AND ONLY BOOK, NOVELIST MARGARET MITCHELL NOT ONLY CREATED ONE OF THE CENTURY'S MOST COLORFUL FICTIONAL HEROINES—SPUNKY, SPIRITED SCARLETT O'HARA— she offered a portrait of the American South that has done more to shape the world's view of that region than dozens of books by far more skilled (not to mention more clear-eyed) writers. ¶ *Gone with the Wind,* Mitchell's mythic, grandly sentimental romance of the Civil War, was released in the deep Depression year of 1936. By year's end, the book had sold some 1.4 million copies, including more than 50,000 on one record-setting day alone. ¶ David O. Selznick's 1939 movie version, which had a spectacular premiere in Atlanta ("To Georgia, it was like winning the Battle of Atlanta 75 years late," *Time* magazine noted wryly), brought millions more into the fold. Starring Clark Gable as the dashing Rhett Butler and relatively unknown British actress Vivien Leigh as Scarlett, *GWTW* garnered 8 Academy Awards and shattered all existing box-office records. ¶ Mitchell grew up in Atlanta society and was weaned on fables of Southern heroism. She was 10 years old, she later joked, before she learned that the South had lost the Civil War. She began shaping these childhood stories into a novel in 1926, when an ankle injury forced her to retire from her feature-writing job at *The Atlanta Journal.* ¶ Mitchell's opus might never have seen print at all had it not been for some gentle arm-twisting from friends, who urged her to give the manuscript to a New York editor who was in Atlanta in 1935 on a talent-scouting mission. He received the manuscript as he was departing for the West Coast; by the time he got there, he'd decided to publish it. ¶ In a tragic coda to her novel's extraordinary fortunes, Mitchell died in 1949 after being struck by a car as she crossed an Atlanta street with her husband.

 It is basically just a simple yarn of fairly simple people. "

margaret

Mitchell

toni Morrison

1931—

> **I'm not *just* a black writer, but categories like black writer, woman writer, and Latin-American writer aren't marginal anymore.**

AFTER RECEIVING THE 1993 NOBEL PRIZE FOR LITERATURE, NOVELIST TONI MORRISON FELT, SHE SAID, "as if the whole category of 'female writer' and 'black writer' had been redeemed." An African-American woman writing from within the black experience, Morrison helped open American letters to what she called "a whole world of women who were either silenced or who had never received the imprimatur of the established literary world." With the Nobel, that missing imprimatur was finally granted. Moreover, the kind of recognition Morrison's lyrical, historically informed novels received helped open commercial publishing to black women novelists, such as Terry McMillan, who write largely for popular audiences. ¶ Morrison's first novel, *The Bluest Eye* (1970) was, in her words, about "the absolute destruction of human life because of the most superficial thing in the world—physical beauty." Based partly on its author's experience of growing up amid Depression-era poverty and prejudice in Lorain, Ohio, *The Bluest Eye* has as its protagonist a teenage black girl who yearns for Caucasian features, especially blue eyes. Morrison, a divorcée, wrote the book at night and on weekends while raising two sons alone and working as a book editor. ¶ After winning the prestigious National Book Critics Circle Award in 1978 for *Song of Solomon*, an examination of African-American folklore from the point of view of a man much like her own grandfather, Morrison began writing full time. One result was the author's masterwork, *Beloved*, a novel of terrible beauty in which a brutalized slave murders her infant daughter rather than deliver her to a life of certain degradation. The book, which won the 1988 Pulitzer Prize for fiction, splendidly showcases the author's virtuosic use of language—language that, as the Nobel committee observed, "addresses us with the luster of poetry."

dorothy
Parker

1893-1967

DOROTHY PARKER STANDS OUT AS THE WITTIEST AND MOST URBANE OF THE LEGENDARY CIRCLE OF ACID-TONGUED JAZZ-AGE WITS KNOWN AS THE ALGONQUIN Round Table (named after the Manhattan hotel where, in 1919, the group began meeting for regular alcohol-drenched lunches). Famous for her light verse ("Men seldom make passes/At girls who wear glasses") and the acerbic book and theater reviews she contributed to *Vanity Fair* and *The New Yorker*, Parker elevated the wisecrack to a minor art form. When a date told her he couldn't bear fools, she replied, "That's odd, your mother could." Another young man was deemed a "rhinestone in the rough." But as deliciously memorable as Parker's put-downs are, they tend to obscure her real influence. In a male-dominated literary world, Parker not only carved out a central position for women of wit (she is constantly cited as a role model for such latter-day humorists as Fran Lebowitz and Nora Ephron), she took the very subjects that male writers scorned as frivolous and portrayed them in a scathing, decidedly unsentimental light. Just beneath the polished surface and Smart Set trappings of her best work lurks a deadly serious theme—exploitation, specifically of women by men. ¶ Parker had plenty of personal experience to draw on, including an early divorce, failed affairs, several suicide attempts, and a torturous, soap-opera-like marriage to actor-writer Alan Campbell, a bisexual many years her junior with whom she collaborated on Hollywood screenplays. Typically, she masked her pain with brittle jokes, washed down with copious quantities of alcohol. Her wit never deserted her. "Promise me," she said to playwright Lillian Hellman, days before she died, "that my gravestone will carry only these words: 'If you can read this, you're too close.'"

**What
fresh hell
is this?**

1932—1963 SYLVIA PLATH'S REPUTATION AS A KIND OF AVENGING ANGEL OF FEMINISM RESTS ALMOST ENTIRELY ON A SERIES OF INTENSE, TAUT, ALMOST HALLUCINATORY POEMS SHE COMPLETED IN THE eight months immediately preceding her 1963 suicide. ¶ Brimming with anger—at the false selves she has lived with, at the men she has served (including her long-dead father and her estranged husband, the acclaimed English poet Ted Hughes)—the poems, which were published posthumously in the volume *Ariel*, possess a near-incantatory power. They seem to have bubbled up from somewhere deep within, expressing thoughts, emotions, and desires ordinarily left unsaid. "The blood jet is poetry," Plath wrote. "There is no stopping it." ¶ Plath had long been writing verse, but before *Ariel*, she specialized mostly in well-wrought, somewhat academic little poems. Always an assiduous student bent on achievement, she had received several literary awards at Smith, where she graduated near the top of her class. But even then the outward golden girl was deeply troubled, suffering a breakdown and suicide attempt after her junior year. (The ordeal was the subject of her 1963 novel, *The Bell Jar*.) ¶ She met Hughes —her "violent Adam" and "the only man in the world who is my match"—in 1955 at England's Cambridge University, where she was studying on a fellowship. They married the following year, full of high-minded intentions of devoting themselves to poetry and the joint nurturing of their poetic gifts. ¶ His career took off first. Plath acted as his stenographer and promoter, began a family (a daughter, born in 1960, a son in 1962), and wrote during whatever time was left. ¶ It was after Hughes began an affair with another woman that her life began unraveling. She mustered the resources to write the *Ariel* poems—a development, Hughes would later say, "that has hardly any equal on record for suddenness and completeness"— but on February 11, 1963, the outpouring stopped. Dragged down by domestic duties and one of the worst English winters in history, Plath put her head in the kitchen oven and turned on the gas. Those final fierce and original poems have been an inspiration to writers—especially young ones, especially women—ever since.

> **Dying is an art, like everything else./ I do it exceptionally well.**
>
> *[from lady lazarus]*

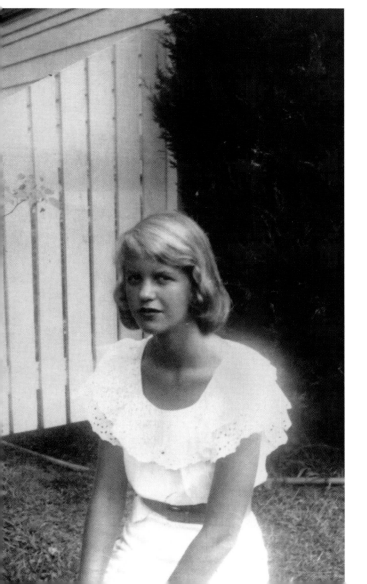

s y l v i a
Plath

gertrude Stein

1874 — 1946 THE INFLUENCE THAT GERTRUDE STEIN CONTINUES TO WIELD MORE THAN 50 YEARS AFTER HER DEATH DERIVES LESS FROM HER OWN FORMIDABLE BODY OF WORK THAN FROM the work of those she championed—among them the most important artistic and literary figures of the century. Stein was the great Sphinx of her artistically tumultuous era—a celebrated writer whose later works were all but unintelligible; a collector of art who was scorned by some of the painters she cultivated; a salon hostess and patron who was so dominant she became the subject of everyone's conversation; a patriotic American who lived abroad her entire adult life. ¶ After dropping out of Harvard one class short of her medical degree, Stein moved to Paris in 1903 with her beloved brother Leo, who was passionately interested in modern art. Made comfortable by a family trust, the Steins began amassing works by then-obscure masters—Picasso, Cézanne, Gauguin, Renoir, Rousseau, Matisse, Braque. Soon the most notable painters, musicians, and writers of the era were flocking to the Steins' apartment to hear Gertrude hold forth on every conceivable topic. ¶ In 1909, Stein met Alice B. Toklas, the American cooking writer and gourmet who became her secretary, lover, and constant companion. When Leo moved out, Toklas moved in. All the while, Stein continued her literary experiments. Her most accessible books are *Three Lives*, a 1909 collection of novellas about economically disadvantaged women, and *The Autobiography of Alice B. Toklas,* a 1933 memoir written by Stein as if from Toklas's point of view. ¶ During World War I, Stein drove up and down the lines in an old Ford station wagon, delivering medical equipment to field hospitals. After the war, she became an object of adoration of the American literary expatriates then streaming into Paris, including Ernest Hemingway, F. Scott Fitzgerald, and Ezra Pound. "You are all a lost generation," she famously told Hemingway, a writer whose clipped, elliptical prose clearly reflects the influence of Stein's own blunt, repetitive style ("a rose is a rose is a rose is a rose" is another famous Stein phrase). Her description would come to emblemize the era.

It takes

a lot of time

to be a genius—

you have to

sit around

so much

doing nothing,

really doing

nothing.

1927— IN A GOOD INTERVIEW, BARBARA WALTERS ONCE TOLD *LADIES' HOME JOURNAL,* IT'S NOT THE FIRST QUESTION THAT MATTERS MOST BUT THE SECOND: "Why do you say that? Why do you feel that?" Walters would know: She has successfully interviewed more famous people—from Hollywood legends to prime ministers, presidents, and kings—than perhaps any journalist in history, man *or* woman. And for better or worse, her intimate style, her unabashed way of asking personal questions of public figures (and getting revealing answers in return), has changed the nature of interview journalism itself. ¶ Walters broke into the national news business as a writer. She moved to NBC's *Today* show in 1961 and began doing on-air reporting. As a "Today Girl," her segments were largely limited to "feminine" subjects—cooking, exercise, fashion. Small wonder that the future interviewer of Anwar Sadat and Fidel Castro felt frustrated. She was promoted to full-fledged cohost in 1974, but even then, during political interviews, was allowed to ask a question only after her partner, Frank McGee, had asked three. ¶ In 1976, Walters made a career move that sent shock waves through the industry: Jumping to ABC, she simultaneously became television's first journalist to command a million-dollar salary and the first female co-anchor of a network evening news program. Subjected to endless scrutiny from the press and overt hostility from her coanchor, Harry Reasoner, Walters has called this period "the most painful in my life." At ABC, she also launched the series that remains her trademark: *The Barbara Walters Special.* Over the years she has talked to every U.S. president since Johnson, such world leaders as Sadat, Castro, Menachem Begin, and Margaret Thatcher, and countless entertainment figures. ¶ Walters has been criticized for being too "soft," for worshipping celebrity, and for crossing the line between journalism and entertainment. But her achievement is undeniable. More than any other journalist, she opened TV news to women. Before Diane Sawyer, Lesley Stahl, and Jane Pauley, there was Barbara, the intrepid reporter who never met a question she was afraid to ask.

> " I have always been very curious about not only what one's actions were but what makes a person tick. "

barbara

Walters

laura ingalls
Wilder

1867—1957

FOR GENERATIONS OF AMERICAN CHILDREN, THE NOVELS OF LAURA INGALLS WILDER HAVE SERVED AS AN INTRODUCTION BOTH TO LITERATURE AND TO THE HOMESTEADING ERA OF American history. In *Little House on the Prairie* and other young adult classics, Wilder drew on her own experiences to present an unforgettable picture of family life in an age without cars, television, or supermarkets. Five of her nine books won Newbery Medals, the Pulitzer Prize of children's literature. In 1954, the Children's Library Association created the Laura Ingalls Wilder Award for "substantial and lasting contribution" to juvenile fiction. ¶ Wilder was born in a log cabin at the edge of the wilderness in Pepin, Wisconsin. During her youth, the family bounced from one place to another as her father sought work. Wherever they landed—Kansas, Missouri, Minnesota, Iowa, Dakota Territory—Wilder's father would regale her and her blind sister, Mary, with frontier tales—about prowling mountain lions, skirmishes between Indians and white settlers, old-fashioned sledding parties. Such lore became the stuff of her own fiction. ¶ Wilder was teaching in a one-room schoolhouse in DeSmet, South Dakota, when she met a local farmer, Almanzo Wilder. They married and, after traveling widely in search of the right place, eventually settled in the Ozarks. (Their Missouri farm is now a historic landmark.) ¶ Wilder was 65 when, urged on by her daughter, she began to write the books that would become the "Little House" series. *Little House in the Big Woods, Farmer Boy, Little House on the Prairie*, and *On the Banks of Plum Creek* combine dramatic sketches about blizzards, Indian raids, and grasshopper plagues with practical details of frontier life (how to churn butter, bake bread, and braid hair). Today, with some 35 million copies of her original titles in print, it is said that more children learn about the settling of the West from Wilder than from any historian.

No one who has

not homesteaded

can understand

the fascination and

terror of it.

LITTLE HOUSE IN THE BIG WOODS
LAURA INGALLS WILDER

Drawings by HELEN SEWELL

HARPER & BROTHERS ESTABLISHED 1817

"

Women have
served all these
centuries as
looking-glasses
possessing the
magic and
delicious power
of reflecting
the figure of a man
at twice
its normal size.

"

1882—1941 IN MARCH 1941, VIRGINIA WOOLF, IN THE THROES OF DEEP DEPRESSION BROUGHT ON BY HER DISMAY OVER THE OUTBREAK OF WORLD WAR II, FILLED her pockets with stones and walked into the Ouse River, near her home in Sussex, England. At the time, the British writer had attracted a loyal but still relatively small following of readers. Novels such as *Mrs. Dalloway* (1925) and *To the Lighthouse* (1927) were admired by intellectuals as exciting literary experiments: Allusive and free-flowing, her books took creative writing to a hidden, subjective place, examining—and recreating—the fleeting thoughts and private feelings that comprise so much of everyday life. ¶ Today, Woolf stands with James Joyce as one of the great modern innovators, a writer whose shimmering stream-of-consciousness style permanently redrew the boundaries of the novel. Moreover, her work helped create a new critical appreciation for a sensibility that was distinctively female. ¶ But if Woolf's writing has always been identified as *feminine*, it has only more recently been recognized as *feminist*. Her 1929 book-length essay, *A Room of One's Own*, is now regarded as a landmark of feminist thought that paved the way for such later classics as Simone de Beauvoir's *The Second Sex*. ¶ Nothing about Woolf's high Victorian upbringing suggested a future as an iconoclast. A bookish girl, she had the first of a series of mental breakdowns in 1895 when her mother died. After her father died nine years later, she suffered another. ¶ After recovering from mental collapse, Woolf moved with two brothers and her sister, Vanessa, a painter, to the Bloomsbury section of London. There they became the center of the influential Edwardian intellectual community known as the Bloomsbury Group. Among the witty circle were art critic Clive Bell, Vanessa's husband; economist John Maynard Keynes; publisher Leonard Woolf, whom Virginia married in 1912; and writer Vita Sackville West, Virginia's lifelong friend and lover. ¶ In 1917, the Woolfs started their own publishing company, Hogarth Press. In addition to all of Virginia's later writings, they published the early poetry of T.S. Eliot and the first English edition of Freud's work. Liberated from any ordinary constraints imposed by editors and publishers, and financially secure from a family trust, Woolf was free to develop her unique style. The importance of material independence was not lost on her. For women, she wrote in her famous essay, the key to intellectual freedom is "five hundred pounds a year and a room of one's own."

Virginia Woolf has at long last achieved literary due. Here in the 1997 version of her 1925 novel, Mrs. Dalloway, Natascha McElhone *and Lena Headey exchange intimacies.*

virginia Woolf

Doctors & Scientists

"Nothing in life is to be feared;
it is only to be understood"

—Marie Curie

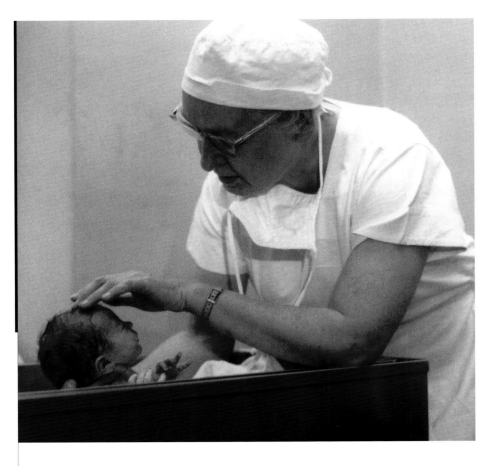

1909—1974

DURING HER DISTINGUISHED CAREER AS AN OBSTETRICS ANESTHESIOLOGIST, DR. VIRGINIA APGAR DIRECTLY ASSISTED IN THE DELIVERY OF some 20,000 babies. But this tribe of Apgar infants represents only a small fraction of the children she helped ease into the world. As the developer of a test used to evaluate the general health of newborns, she has been a spiritual presence in virtually every delivery room around the world since 1952, when the test was introduced. ¶ Elegant in its simplicity, the Apgar Score rates infants on a scale of 0 to 2 on five vital functions—heart rate, respiration, reflex irritability, muscle tone, and skin color. A 0 score indicates no response; 1 is marginal; 2 is ideal. Administered 60 seconds after delivery and again four minutes later, the formula (the first of its kind) enables physicians and midwives to take a quick, accurate reading of an infant's condition—and so to identify and instantly aid a baby who is at risk. ¶ Apgar's inspiration came from observing how, immediately after birth, infants tended to be shunted off to nurseries to be examined later. While birth complications were relatively rare—"you have better than a nine-to-one chance that none of the mishaps described here will happen to *your* baby," she assured readers of *Ladies' Home Journal* in a 1966 article on birth defects—such delays could be disastrous for babies born with medical problems. ¶ Apgar had originally hoped to be a surgeon—she won a rare surgical internship after graduating from medical school—but was advised to change specialties: Women simply did not do surgery. (For the rest of her life, she bemoaned the fact that women "have to be so much better at things than men do to be recognized by society.") She switched to the young field of anesthesiology, becoming one of the country's first 50 licensed anesthesiologists. She went on to become the first female full professor of medicine at Columbia University and, in a second career at the March of Dimes Foundation, a forceful advocate for better prenatal care and the reduction of congenital deformities.

"

Time is of utmost importance. Delay is damaging to the infant. Act promptly, accurately, and gently.

"

v i r g i n i a

Apgar

helen
Caldicott

1938— DR. HELEN CALDICOTT HAS PROBABLY DONE MORE THAN ANY OTHER SINGLE PERSON TO WARN THE WORLD ABOUT THE PERILS OF THE BOMB. HER EFFORTS TO AVERT THE "FINAL EPIDEMIC" OF NUCLEAR WAR HAVE BEEN AS TIRELESS AS HER MOTIVES HAVE BEEN transparent: A mother and pediatrician, she wants to make the world a safer place for her own and every other parent's children. ¶ A native of Australia, Caldicott was a young doctor when, in 1971, she learned that France was testing nuclear weapons in the South Pacific. Her pediatric training had made her well aware of radiation's

dangerous effects, especially on children, and she wrote a letter of protest to her local newspaper. Within days, the mainstream media had picked up the story and Caldicott became the de facto national spokesperson for a budding nuclear disarmament movement—making impassioned, medically informed speeches, organizing demonstrations, leading a boycott of French products. A year later, the French government stopped the illegal tests. ¶ Caldicott continued her fight after moving to Boston with her husband and three young children in 1975. "I was naive to think we could get rid of nuclear weapons," Caldicott has said, "but naiveté gave me the power to do what I do. Other people would have said, 'This is *ridiculous*, taking on the military-industrial complex in the most powerful country on earth,' but the earth's population was at risk." Four years later a near-meltdown at Pennsylvania's Three Mile Island nuclear reactor brought thousands flocking to her cause. ¶ Caldicott's crusade has been waged at enormous personal cost: She gave up her medical practice and professorship at Harvard, surrendered the presidency of Physicians for Social Responsibility (when the advocacy group wanted to soften its position on nuclear power), and watched her 26-year marriage fall victim to her impossible schedule. Caldicott has never looked back. "I couldn't not have done it," she says of her mission. "It's almost the blueprint I was born with. I could feel the heat of the bombs."

marie Curie

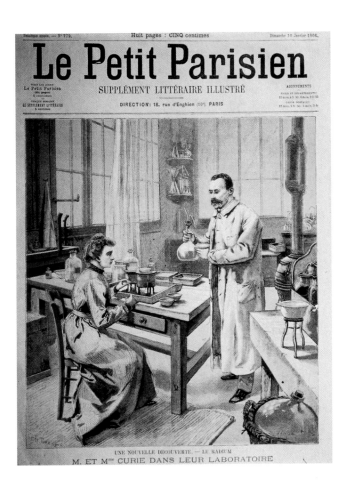

Le Petit Parisien

SUPPLÉMENT LITTÉRAIRE ILLUSTRÉ

DIRECTION: 18, rue d'Enghien (10°), PARIS

UNE NOUVELLE DÉCOUVERTE. — LE RADIUM
M. ET Mme CURIE DANS LEUR LABORATOIRE

[Marie Curie and her husband Pierre made breakthrough discoveries in the field of radioactivity.]

1867 — 1934 DURING HER LIFETIME, MADAME MARIE CURIE WAS THE WORLD'S MOST FAMOUS WOMAN SCIENTIST— AND SO SHE REMAINS TODAY. WITH HER HUSBAND, PIERRE CURIE, AND THE French physicist Henri Becquerel, and later on her own, Curie pioneered the study of radioactivity (a word she coined). ¶ In 1903, the Curies and Becquerel shared the Nobel Prize for physics for their work measuring the radiation of uranium and for discovering two new radioactive elements, polonium and radium. It was the first time a woman had ever won a Nobel. In 1911, Curie became the first and only woman to win two Nobel prizes. She earned, on her own, the award in chemistry for isolating pure radium. ¶ With regard to the chemical elements, the detection of radium is said to be second in importance only to the discovery of oxygen. Curie's work was not only a leaping-off point for the modern field of nuclear medicine, but it helped lay the groundwork for the most important development in 20th-century science—the discovery of the structure of the atom. As great as her scientific achievements were, though, Curie's primary contribution to society may be symbolic: She demonstrated that women could excel in male-dominated fields. ¶ A native of Russian-occupied Poland, Marie Sklodowska moved to Paris in 1891 to study. She earned degrees in physics and mathematics, and married Pierre Curie, a professor of physics. Inspired by Becquerel, who had recently discovered the radioactive properties of uranium, Curie made radiation the subject of her Ph.D. dissertation. Working in a makeshift lab in an outbuilding at Pierre's school, the couple discovered polonium, named for Marie's native Poland, and then radium. (Marie later said that if they had had access to a modern laboratory, the work it took them four years to do could have been accomplished in one.) After Pierre's death in 1906, Marie assumed his chair at the Sorbonne, becoming the first female professor in the university's history. ¶ Both Curies paid a high physical price for their work with radiation—which included a number of experiments in which they burned themselves with radioactive compounds to observe the effects. "Dust, the air of the room, and one's clothes, all become radioactive," Curie noted grimly. Radiation sickness rendered Pierre an invalid before his 1906 accident. Their daughter Irène, their son-in-law, and numerous lab assistants all died or were severely disabled by various radiation-linked diseases. Surprisingly, Marie lived into her sixties, but suffered generally poor health, as well as increasing blindness and deafness, for years before her death from leukemia.

Nothing in life

is to be

feared.

It is only

to be

understood.

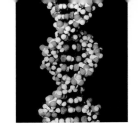

1920–1958

BRILLIANT, BEAUTIFUL, AND FIERCELY SERIOUS ABOUT SCIENCE, BRITISH MOLECULAR BIOLOGIST ROSALIND FRANKLIN WAS ODD WOMAN OUT ON ONE OF THE 20TH CENTURY'S MOST SIGNIFICANT INTELLECTUAL ADVANCES. FRANKLIN'S X-RAY crystallography studies were the key that allowed her more heralded colleagues, James Watson and Francis Crick, to unlock the mystery of deoxyribonucleic acid (DNA), the molecule that carries the genetic information for all living things. For their groundbreaking work, Watson and Crick, along with British biophysicist Maurice Wilkins, received the 1962 Nobel Prize in physiology. By then Franklin was dead of ovarian cancer —a double tragedy because only living scientists can receive the Nobel. ¶ It was in a laboratory in Paris, where she moved after World War II, that Franklin first learned X-ray diffraction, a technique that uses a laser beam to map the atomic structure of crystals. In 1951, she joined a research team studying DNA crystallography at King's College, London. There, her X-ray diffraction photographs provided the most lucid available picture of DNA, and Franklin hoped to untangle its structure. Her research notes reveal that she came tantalizingly close, even noting the molecule's two interlocking chains, but failing to divine the crucial connection between them. ¶ Watson and Crick were shown Franklin's work (without her approval, she later claimed). One glimpse was all they needed: Leaping off from Franklin's meticulous lab results, the intuitive duo came up with their elegant DNA model, consisting of two intertwined, spiraling strands of polymers (a double helix) that, when separated, become the foundation on which an identical new strand is built. ¶ Although Watson's 1968 book about the discovery, *The Double Helix*, largely dismissed her as an uncooperative cog (enraging many in the scientific community), Franklin is now universally recognized for her pivotal role in one of history's most important scientific revolutions—the study of genetics.

> 66
>
> **We are not going to speculate, we are going to wait, we are going to let the spots on this photograph tell us what the structure is.**
>
> 99
>
> *[on the search for the structure of DNA]*

r o s a l i n d

Franklin

jane Goodall

FOR MORE THAN 35 YEARS, ENGLISH ANIMAL BEHAVIORIST JANE GOODALL HAS SERVED AS THE CHIEF MEDIATOR BETWEEN HUMANS AND chimpanzees, *homo sapiens'* closest living relatives. Her work at the Gombe Stream Reserve in Tanzania simultaneously revolutionized the scientific study of animals in the wild and turned human assumptions about lesser primates on their ear. In the assessment of paleontologist Stephen Jay Gould, it is "one of the Western world's great scientific achievements." ¶ Among the key observations first made by Goodall were that chimpanzees are carnivorous; they hunt; they make sounds that approximate language; they engage in warfare; they experience awe at natural wonders like waterfalls; and they make and use tools. This last is one of the most significant discoveries of the century: Tool-making had previously been considered to be a defining characteristic of humans. ¶ Through a series of television shows, magazine articles, and books (significantly 1971's bestselling *In the Shadow of Man*), the retiring scientist became something of a pop culture star—not to mention a professional role model for young men and women who revere her for her dedication and her adventurous spirit. "It's amazing," says a colleague, "how many people entering the field of primatology say they were inspired by Jane." ¶ A long-time conservationist and animal rights activist, Goodall uses her celebrity today to publicize such causes as poaching, the global destruction of wilderness, and the abusive treatment received by medical research animals. But at the center of her activism are her beloved chimps. Alarmed that their population has dwindled from about 2 million in 1900 to about 200,000 scattered in small groups, Goodall travels around the world to get her message out. But, she says wistfully, "spiritually, I've never left Africa."

When I first started at Gombe I thought the chimps were nicer than we are. But time has revealed that they are not. They can be just as awful.

grace Hopper

> **"**
>
> The most
>
> damaging phrase
>
> in the language is
>
> 'We've always
>
> done it this way.'
>
> **"**

1906—1992 GRACE MURRAY HOPPER WAS MIDWIFE TO THE COMPUTER REVOLUTION. AT A TIME WHEN ONLY a handful of people in the world had even conceived of electronic calculating machines, Hopper—known as "Amazing Grace" to admiring colleagues— made several key contributions to the technology that drives today's world. ¶ A career Navy officer, Hopper worked as a programmer on the Harvard-Navy team that in 1944 produced the Mark I, an early prototype of the electronic computer. Less than a decade later, she was involved in the creation of UNIVAC, the first all-purpose, all-electronic digital computer. Brilliant, innovative, endlessly curious, Hopper went on to invent the first computer compiler, a program that translates written instructions into codes that can be read directly by computers. This work led to her codevelopment of COBOL, one of the earliest standardized computer languages. With COBOL, computers were able for the first time to respond to words as well as to numbers. ¶ A native of New York City, Hopper was the first woman to earn a doctorate in mathematics at Yale in 1934. In 1941, she enlisted in the Navy, which, with Harvard, was developing the Mark I to generate the ballistics tables used to aim naval guns. ¶ Hopper was put in charge of programming the room-sized machine. With some 750,000 parts and 500 miles of electrical wire, the Mark I was a contemporary marvel, able to solve in a day calculations that would otherwise have taken as long as six months. It was during her work on the Mark I that Hopper coined the term "bug" to describe a computer glitch. Checking wiring one day after the computer had mysteriously stopped working, Hopper discovered that a moth was wedged in a relay. She extricated the insect with a pair of tweezers and pasted it in a logbook, making the handwritten notation, "First actual case of a bug being found." The term stuck. ¶ After retiring from active service in 1946, Hopper became one of the world's foremost computing prophets, giving as many as 300 lectures a year about a here-to-stay technology that would one day, she confidently predicted, be small enough and inexpensive enough to sit on the desktops of people who were not professional programmers.

> 66
>
> Allowance
>
> must be made
>
> for the great
>
> difficulty of
>
> expressing
>
> a young child's
>
> feelings and
>
> fantasies in
>
> adult language.
>
> 99

1882—1960

WITH "PLAY THERAPY," AUSTRIAN-BORN BRITISH PSYCHOANALYST MELANIE KLEIN CREATED A MEANS TO ANALYZE A GROUP largely ignored by Freud—small children who are too young to articulate their feelings. Klein believed that children bare their souls by acting out symbolic scenarios with toys in much the same way that adults reveal deep-seated impulses by free-associating under a psychoanalyst's guidance. By observing her tiny patients—sometimes as young as one—playing with toys representing mother, father, and siblings, Klein was able to surmise their unconscious fears and desires. Her methods remain fundamental to child psychology today. ¶ Long before she postulated that infants experience birth as a violent assault, Klein was herself enduring an unhappy childhood in Vienna. Her mother was domineering, her father, a doctor who turned to dentistry because he couldn't attract patients in anti-Semitic Austria, remote and authoritarian. One brother took his own life. Her own unhappy marriage produced three children, including a son who died in a hiking accident and a daughter who became an analyst—and one of her mother's harshest professional critics. ¶ Klein initially encountered psychoanalysis as a patient. While living in Budapest, she had come across Freud's 1901 study, *On Dreams*. Intrigued by the idea of the unconscious and depressed by her mother's death, she began analysis with Sandor Ferenczi, a disciple of Freud. Their sessions soon evolved into tutorials, with Ferenczi urging Klein to take up the analysis of children. ¶ As a theorist Klein eventually came to rival Freud, the master from whom she increasingly deviated. Orthodox Freudians still quibble with many of her ideas—she contended, for instance, that the developmental stages identified by Freud (oral, anal, phallic, and genital) occur simultaneously in a child's first year—but about her seminal role in child psychology there is no dispute whatsoever.

melanie

Klein

Mary Leakey with her husband Louis studying skull fragments in Tangayika. The couple had been sifting the fossil-rich rocks for more than 25 years.

mary

Leakey

> "
> Theories
>
> come and go,
>
> but fundamental
>
> data always
>
> remain
>
> the same.
> "

1913—1996 BEGINNING IN THE 1930S, MARY LEAKEY, MATRIARCH OF THE FAMOUS LEAKEY FAMILY OF FOSSIL HUNTERS, MADE A SERIES OF ARCHAEOLOGICAL discoveries that fundamentally altered the way we view human evolution. Among the most spectacular finds were two skulls and a telltale set of footprints. The skulls, uncovered in 1948 and 1959, traced the origins of human life to Africa (not Asia, as previously assumed). The trail of fossilized footprints, found in 1978 and dated to 3.6 million years, proved conclusively that hominids began to walk upright far earlier than scientists had believed. ¶ Although Leakey's colorful husband Louis largely provided the public face for the family's groundbreaking work, it was Mary who supplied the rigorous science. "Louis was always the better publicist," said the couple's son Richard, himself a fossil hunter of considerable repute. "But Mary was the centerpiece of the research." ¶ Mary Nicol was a failed student ("I had never passed a single exam in my life," she later wrote), amateur archaeologist, and part-time illustrator in 1933, when she fell in love with Louis Leakey, a Cambridge University archaeologist already renowned for his work in East Africa. In a scandal that would cost Louis his professorship, the couple began living together before he divorced his first wife. After marrying in 1936, they set off for Olduvai Gorge, in Tanzania. ¶ There Mary Leakey lived and worked for the better part of the next half-century. While Louis often traveled abroad to raise money for their expeditions, she remained quite literally in the trenches, digging up fossils, bones, and stone tools, and carefully sketching and cataloguing her finds. Her meticulous work helped set scientific standards for excavation and documentation that prevail today. ¶ By the late 1960s, the Leakeys had separated, in part because of Louis's chronic infidelity, in part because his weakness for fanciful theories offended the cautious scientist in Mary. ¶ "Compelled by curiosity," as she wrote in her autobiography, Leakey was passionate about her work until the end. "Given the chance," she told an interviewer not long before her death, "I'd rather be in a tent than a house."

1902—1992 BARBARA MCCLINTOCK WAS ONE OF THOSE RARE GENIUSES SO FAR AHEAD OF THEIR TIME THAT A GENERATION OR TWO MUST PASS BEFORE THEIR BRILLIANCE can be fully recognized. McClintock's research on corn showed that certain genetic elements, far from being fixed, can move around on the chromosomes and thereby alter genetic material from one generation to the next. This discovery was recognized with a 1983 Nobel Prize for medicine; McClintock had made the discovery nearly 40 years earlier. ¶ Counted today among history's three most important geneticists (Gregor Mendel, who discovered heredity, and Thomas Hunt Morgan, who used fruit flies to demonstrate its physical basis, are the other two of "the three Ms"), McClintock was largely ignored, even ridiculed, when she first began publishing her "jumping gene" theory. It was far easier for the scientific community to marginalize McClintock than it was to admit that a lone woman knew more than all the other experts combined. ¶ McClintock was unperturbed by the lack of recognition. It allowed her to devote more time to her research. But not courting fame was one thing. Being written off because of her sex was another. ¶ In 1936, a furious McClintock quit her job in the biology department of the University of Missouri after the chairman told her that she would never be hired as a full professor, and that if her mentor left, she would be fired. At the time, she was vice president of the Genetics Society of America (she would later serve as the first female president), and only a few years away from becoming the third woman ever elected to the National Academy of Sciences. For five years McClintock bounced around from job to job, always working with maize, her plant of choice. Then, in 1941, the Carnegie Institution offered her the position of her dreams, complete with a cornfield, a laboratory, a home (two rooms over a garage), and no requirement to teach or lecture, or do anything else but research. She proceeded to do just that for 12 hours a day, 6 days a week, for 50 years.

barbara

McClintock

66

When you know

you're right,

you don't care.

You can't be hurt.

You just know,

sooner or later,

it will come out

in the wash,

but you may have

to wait some time.

99

THE BRILLIANT AUSTRIAN PHYSICIST LISE MEITNER, WHO FIRST CALCULATED THE ENERGY LIBERATED BY SPLITTING THE ATOM, REPRESENTS the ability of a strong woman to overcome long odds—odds that included anti-Semitism as well as institutional sexism—in pursuit of the highest goals. ¶ In the 1930s, Meitner and her long-time collaborator and close friend, German chemist Otto Hahn, carried out the nuclear experiments that led to the development of both the atomic bomb and nuclear power. In 1938, Hahn forwarded their results to Meitner in Stockholm. (Like other Jewish scientists working in Germany, she had been forced to flee after Hitler invaded Austria that same year.)¶ It was Meitner, working in Sweden with her nephew, physicist Otto Frisch, who studied the experiments and figured out how a uranium atom splits and releases massive quantities of energy after being bombarded with neutrons. Coining the term "fission" for this process, she and Frisch explained it in a groundbreaking 1939 article in the journal *Nature*. From that point, the development of an atomic bomb became, to Meitner's everlasting dismay, an inevitability. ¶ She remained in Sweden throughout the war, refusing an invitation to become part of the Manhattan Project to develop a bomb. After a fission device was used to bomb Hiroshima in 1945, Meitner told *The Saturday Evening Post*, "You must not blame us scientists for the use to which war technicians have put our discoveries." ¶ Despite Meitner's key role in the identification of fission, she was overlooked for the 1944 Nobel Prize for chemistry, which went to Hahn. A breach occurred between the two (who had once enjoyed an almost spouselike closeness)—not because Meitner was snubbed by the Nobel committee, but because Hahn and his colleagues had failed to stand up to Hitler. "You have all worked for Nazi Germany and you never once even attempted a passive resistance," she wrote to Hahn. "[Y]ou let millions of innocent people be murdered." ¶ After the war, Meitner not only penetrated the male fraternity of nuclear physics during its heyday, she occupied a central place within it for some 30 years. Throughout, she steadfastly refused to use her knowledge to build weapons. "My hope," she said after Hiroshima, "is that the atomic bomb will make humanity realize that we must, once and for all, finish with war."

My hope is that

the atomic bomb

will make

humanity realize

that we must,

once and for all,

finish with war.

lise Meitner

Entrepre

neurs

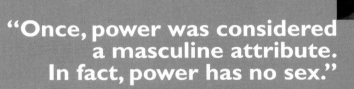

"Once, power was considered
a masculine attribute.
In fact, power has no sex."

—Katharine Graham

coco Chanel

> **"**
>
> **How many**
>
> **cares one loses**
>
> **when one**
>
> **decides not to**
>
> **be something**
>
> **but to be**
>
> **someone.**
>
> **"**

1883—1971 BY FREEING HAUTE COUTURE FROM ITS FUSTY, 19TH-CENTURY STYLES, GABRIELLE "COCO" CHANEL FREED WOMEN themselves. Her innovations, which helped obliterate Victorian notions of femininity, are now essential elements in the basic vocabulary of fashion: faux pearls, trench coats, simple knits, turtleneck sweaters, the "little black dress." Her signature suit—a collarless cardigan jacket trimmed in braid and an elegantly straight skirt—is the single most-copied fashion design of all time. ¶ But Chanel was also a shrewd entrepreneur who grasped early on the value of spinning off her name. In 1921, she launched a fragrance and called it, simply, Chanel No. 5. That fragrance—still one of the world's most popular—became the cornerstone of an empire that, at its height in the late 1920s, employed some 3,500 people. ¶ Born into a French peasant family, Chanel ran off with a cavalry officer at 16; at 20, with the backing of a paramour, she was a milliner in Paris. In 1913, as the 30-year-old mistress of an English businessman, she opened a boutique in the trendy resort of Deauville. Almost at once, her elegant, uncomplicated designs began to alter the way women of style looked and dressed. ¶ "Her first customers were princesses and duchesses," legendary *Vogue* editor

Diana Vreeland said, "and she dressed them like secretaries and stenographers." And, indeed, while her client list included the world's wealthiest women, it was these "working girls"—the millions of women who began moving into the workplace in the 1920s—whom Chanel claimed as her natural constituency. With her urging, these women cut their hair and discarded their uncomfortable bone corsets.¶ Chanel closed her couture house during World War II, but remained in Paris, living with a Nazi officer. Reviled as a collaborator after the war, she fled to Switzerland. She returned to Paris triumphantly in 1954 and ran her couture house until her death. ¶ Chanel was the best designer of her time, she liked to say, because she had "lived the life of the century." For women today, however, Chanel's most enduring contribution rests on a simple, yet radical, proposition: She proved it possible to be comfortable and chic at the same time.

"

Some people like to paint pictures, or do gardening, or build a boat in the basement. Other people get a tremendous pleasure out of the kitchen, because cooking is just as creative and imaginative an activity as drawing, or wood carving, or music.

"

1912—

BACK BEFORE THE UNITED STATES BECAME A NATION OF AMATEUR GOURMETS and food hobbyists, before it gave up iceberg lettuce for escarole, instant pudding for crème brulée, Julia Child quite literally wrote the book on sophisticated home cooking. It was called *Mastering the Art of French Cooking*, and its appearance back in 1961 triggered the "foodie" revolution that is still in progress. Every specialty food shop, every gourmet section of the supermarket, every cooking show on cable is a direct descendant of Child and that first groundbreaking book. ¶ Child got the idea for *Mastering* while living in France in the 1950s with her husband Paul Child, a sophisticated American painter turned foreign service officer who was 10 years her senior. Hearty eaters both, the couple relished good meals together, especially classic French cuisine, all cream sauces and roasted meats. (To this day, Child is unapologetic about her liberal use of butter, eggs, and cream. What's the sense of eating, she wonders, if it doesn't *taste* good?) But Child, a wholly inexperienced cook, struggled in the kitchen. Most cookbooks, she complained, were of little use. ¶ Child overcame her kitchen phobia by enrolling in France's esteemed Cordon Bleu culinary institute, but realized that most women needed a more practical option. Six years of research later, she produced *Mastering*. "My idea is," she said, "if you read one of my recipes, you really know how to do it." ¶ Published when its author was 49, the book became an immediate sensation in the United States, and so did Child herself after she showed up for a public television interview with a hot plate, a bowl, and some eggs, and proceeded to whip up a soufflé. The producer was so impressed that he created a new program, *The French Chef,* just for her. ¶ With her great size and now-famous fluttery voice, the irrepressible Child was an unlikely TV star—all the more popular because she never intimidated or browbeat viewers. Nearly four decades later, her books and television shows continue to find an audience of millions.

julia **Child**

> A woman's environment will speak for her life, whether she likes it or not... A house is a dead giveaway.

elsie de Wolfe

1865—1950 ELSIE DE WOLFE, THE COUNTRY'S FIRST PROFESSIONAL INTERIOR DECORATOR AND A SELF-APPOINTED ARBITER OF DOMESTIC TASTE, CHANGED THE WAY AMERICANS LIVED. AT A TIME WHEN THE WELL-TO-DO FAVORED DARK PANELED WALLS, HEAVY velvet drapes, and bric-a-brac clutter, de Wolfe adopted a very different aesthetic credo: "I believe," she said, "in plenty of optimism and white paint." The style she first delineated—light interiors, delicate antiques, bright cotton chintz fabrics—remains central to American interior design. ¶ De Wolfe was an internationally regarded actress who retired from the stage in 1905 upon realizing she was "no Sarah Bernhardt." She set about remodeling the modest New York City townhouse she shared with the high-powered literary agent Elizabeth Marbury. Already the most famous lesbian couple in New York, de Wolfe and Marbury became even better known once their home was made over. Members of the smart set— who gathered at the couple's salon—adored the light, antiques-filled space de Wolfe created. As word spread, de Wolfe began receiving private commissions. The wealthy, she discovered, would pay handsomely to make their homes tasteful. They just needed someone to tell them how. ¶ De Wolfe preached that "good taste" (a term she popularized) was a matter of sensibility, not money. Her 1913 book, *The House in Good Taste*, brought her message to the masses. ¶ In 1926, the sixtyish de Wolfe married Sir Charles Mendl, an affable British aristocrat. As Lady Mendl, de Wolfe entertained her guests by doing headstands at dinner parties. She also tinted her graying hair in shades of pink or blue (giving rise to the phenomenon of blue-haired ladies). ¶ With her fresh sense of color and light, De Wolfe launched the country's ongoing love affair with stylish living and delivered American homes into the 20th century.

katharine
Graham

1917— WHEN PHILIP GRAHAM, THE PRESIDENT AND PUBLISHER OF THE *WASHINGTON POST*, COMMITTED SUICIDE IN 1963, FEW OBSERVERS WOULD HAVE GUESSED THAT HIS SHY, GRIEF-STRICKEN, 46-YEAR-OLD WIDOW WOULD NOT ONLY STEP INTO HER HUSBAND'S job, but that she would do it so capably, and with such passion and courage, that the sleepy local paper would grow into one of the world's most respected dailies, with a power sufficient to topple the President of the United States. Yet the perennially underestimated Katharine Graham did exactly that. ¶ The first major test of her mettle came in 1971, when she published sections of the Pentagon Papers, a classified government study detailing decades of U.S. ineptitude in Southeast Asia—even though President Richard Nixon's Justice Department had slapped *The New York Times* with an injunction for doing the same. (The Supreme Court ultimately sided with the newspapers.) A scant year later, Graham gave *Post* reporters Carl Bernstein and Bob Woodward the go-ahead to pursue the then-embryonic Watergate scandal to wherever it led. In doing so, she faced the raw hostility of some of the world's most powerful men. ("Katie Graham is gonna get her tit caught in a big fat wringer," Nixon's attorney general, John Mitchell, famously threatened. Graham would not be cowed, saying, "I never killed a story in my life.") The trail led all the way to the White House. The *Post*'s coverage of the Watergate scandal as it unraveled—and as other news organizations dragged their feet—resulted in a Pulitzer Prize in 1973. A year later Nixon resigned as the nation's 37th president. ¶ Over the years, Graham contended with sexism, the second-guessing of her employees, the resentment of her social peers, and her own guilt over being a career woman instead of a full-time mother. ("No matter which choice is made," she told *Ladies' Home Journal* in 1984, "the trade-offs are absolutely enormous.") Yet in 1993, when she stepped down as chair of the Washington Post Company, her wise stewardship had not only secured the paper's blue-chip reputation, it had turned the company into a $1.85 billion empire whose assets include *Newsweek* magazine and cable TV stations around the country. In 1998, at 80, this quintessential late bloomer added yet another accolade to her impressive collection: Her autobiography, *Personal History*, was awarded the Pulitzer Prize for biography.

> My daughter and
> her friends were
> using paper dolls
> to reflect
> the adult world
> around them.
> I used to watch
> that over and over
> and think:
> If only we could
> take this play
> pattern and three-
> dimensionalize it,
> we would have
> something
> very special.

FOR BETTER OR WORSE, AN ANATOMICALLY IMPROBABLE MOLDED PLASTIC STATUETTE NAMED BARBIE HAS BECOME A UNIVERSAL ICON—SO FAMILIAR that it barely seems to have been invented at all. But Barbie is a patented commodity created by the California entrepreneur Ruth Handler, who in 1945 cofounded with her husband, Elliot, the company that would become Mattel. The couple had produced hit toys before Barbie, but none so lasting or so profitable. By the mid-1990s, Handler's brainchild was selling to the tune of $2 billion a year. ¶ Handler got the idea for a vinyl figure with an adult-shaped body from watching her daughter, Barbara, play with paper dolls. Barbara's games of make-believe—she preferred the teenager or career women cutouts, her mother noticed, to the babies or children—convinced Handler that girls used dolls to act out future roles. "When I conceived Barbie," Handler wrote in her 1995 autobiography, *Dream Doll*, "I believed it was important to a little girl's self-esteem to play with a doll that has breasts." (Many contemporary critics argue the opposite—that Barbie's stupendous measurements, which were finally made more realistic in 1998, can trigger body-image insecurities in girls who will never be as thin or, paradoxically, as curvaceous as their plaything.) ¶ Named after the Handlers' daughter and loosely based on a racy German comic-book character named Lilli, the Barbie doll made her debut at the 1959 toy fair in New York City. By that summer Barbie had rocketed to the top of every American girl's wish list. (The Handlers' son, Kenneth, would get his own namesake two years later when Mattel introduced a boyfriend for Barbie.) ¶ Four decades later, the Barbie doll is available in 140 countries around the world, and sells at the astonishing rate of two dolls every second. In the 1990s, a typical American girl between the ages of 3 and 10 owns an average of eight Barbies, and Barbie herself has metamorphosed into identities as diverse as Baywatch Barbie, Barbie the veterinarian, and Barbie as Dorothy in the Wizard of Oz.

r u t h

Handler

THE BUSINESS OF BEAUTY IS HARD WORK. SUCH IS THE LESSON IMPARTED BY COSMETICS MAGNATE ESTÉE LAUDER. BORN JOSEPHINE ESTHER MENTZER TO IMMIGRANTS FROM Eastern Europe in or around 1908 (Lauder refuses to divulge the exact date), the future beauty empress made her professional start during the Depression, when, as a young housewife, she began selling an uncle's home-brew face creams in New York City beauty parlors. ("Hope in a jar" is what Lauder called her uncle's concoctions.) ¶ Lauder's uncle, a professional chemist, never realized much profit from his skin-care inventions, which, in his niece's words, "made your face feel like spun silk." Meanwhile, the enterprising Lauder built her business into Estée Lauder Inc., founded in 1946 with her husband Joe Lauder. Today the family-run business (which went public in 1995 after decades of private ownership) sells perfume, makeup, and face treatments to the tune of well beyond $3 billion a year. There is hardly a woman alive today—in the United States or in the 70-odd countries where Lauder products are sold—who has not sampled or considered sampling her company's wares. ¶ Lauder has prospered by recognizing the value of loyalty. When competitors marketed their products in pharmacies, she stuck with the more upscale department stores. The strategy produced two tangible results: It helped create an aura of exclusivity, and it made Lauder essential to the department stores, where today the line accounts for nearly 40 percent of all cosmetics and perfume sales. But Lauder's single greatest innovation may well be her practice of giving away free product samples with purchases. Established retailers sniffed at the idea—until they saw the return business it generated. Now the complimentary gift is a cosmetics industry staple.

This may be the only country in the world where the work ethic marches hand in hand with the beauty and style ethic.

estée

Lauder

jean Nidetch

> **You have to make the decision to lose weight in your head, not your stomach.**

1923—

BACK IN 1961, JEAN NIDETCH WAS AN OVERWEIGHT HOUSEWIFE FROM QUEENS, NEW YORK, WHEN SHE MADE A LIFE-CHANGING DISCOVERY: STAYING ON A DIET WAS EASIER WHEN YOU shared the experience with others in the same boat. ¶ Nidetch had been shocked into dieting after being asked when her baby was due. The only problem: She wasn't pregnant. Desperately unhappy with her 214-pound figure, Nidetch—who'd been trying to lose weight for years—contacted the Obesity Clinic at the New York City Department of Health and was given a diet developed by Dr. Norman Jolliffe. The program—low-fat proteins and plenty of fruits and vegetables— worked, but Nidetch found herself constantly cheating. ¶ To boost her morale, she invited six other dieting women to meet once a week in her living room for tea (no cream) and sympathy. Within a year, Nidetch had dropped 72 pounds, going from, as she put it, "a perfect size 44 to an imperfect size 12." Other members had equally dramatic results (Nidetch's husband, a bus driver, also shed 70 pounds). When the group got too large for Nidetch's home, she began charging $2 admission to cover the cost of renting a meeting hall. ¶ In 1963, less than two years after starting her informal dieters' club, a trim and newly confident Nidetch incorporated Weight Watchers International. Within five years, Weight Watchers had close to 100 franchises and was helping millions lose weight with its tried-and-true technique—Dr. Jolliffe's sensible eating plan, modest membership dues (a virtue that made the program accessible to ordinary middle- and working-class women), and lots of group support. In 1978, when Nidetch sold the company to H.J. Heinz, the food conglomerate, for $71.2 million, Weight Watchers was doing business in 40 states and overseas. ¶ Today, its meetings are attended by approximately a million people a week in 24 countries. The core diet has been modified, but its basic formula remains unchanged. "Lots of people felt like they were the only ones with a weight problem," says Nidetch. "I said to people in Italy, England, Australia, Canada, and many other countries, 'You're not alone.'"

mary Quant

" Good taste
is death;
vulgarity life. "

1934— TWO DEVELOPMENTS BEYOND ALL OTHERS REVOLUTIONIZED WOMEN'S FASHION IN THE 20TH CENTURY. THE FIRST WAS THE NYLON STOCKING, MADE POSSIBLE BY NEW TECHNOLOGY. THE SECOND WAS THE miniskirt, popularized in 1965 by young British designer and boutique owner Mary Quant. The mini allowed women, in Quant's words, "to dance, to move, to be." Thirty-five years after first raising eyebrows, the mini still stands for liberation—of high fashion from hidebound old couture houses; of youth from parental restriction; of female sexuality from its historical confinement to the boudoir. ¶ Quant knew nothing about the fashion business when she and her future husband Alexander Plunket Greene opened a hip clothing shop called Bazaar in London's Chelsea in 1955. What the recent art-school graduate did know was that the times were changing—and that she "wanted the young to have fashions of their own." The petite, dark-haired Quant soon gave them those fashions: brightly colored thigh-high skirts, patterned bell-bottoms, lacy black tights—the quintessential "London Look" of the 1960s. Other couturiers had created most of the designs (Courrèges actually introduced the first miniskirt), but it was Quant who infused them with the energy of the rock-and-roll subculture and, by availing herself of mass production, actually made it possible for the young to afford them. "Once only the rich, the Establishment set the fashion," she said, proudly claiming her constituency. "Now it is the inexpensive little dress seen on the girls in the High Street." ¶ Bazaar soon became the epicenter of mod London. The Beatles shopped there, as did Brigitte Bardot and Elizabeth Taylor. Perhaps Quant's most visionary stroke was to design her products (which eventually included household items as well), then license the designs—an enormously lucrative marketing technique that spawned dozens of later imitators. By 1966, Quant was a household name, her signature style a respected commodity sold in hundreds of shops throughout the world. That year, Queen Elizabeth awarded her the Order of the British Empire, which Quant received wearing—what else?—a hip-hugging mini.

[*Mary Quant and her husband Alexander Plunket Greene (in their London flat, 1967) started their fashion empire with a clothing shop in Chelsea.*]

I'm only
trying to make
people's lives
a little more
pleasing
to them.

martha Stewart

1941— WHAT DISTINGUISHES MARTHA STEWART FROM SUCH EARLIER
DOMESTIC DOYENNES AS ELSIE DE WOLFE OR JULIA CHILD IS THE
BREADTH OF HER EXPERTISE—EVERYTHING FROM ENTERTAINING TO GARDENING TO CRAFTS
to home decor—and her nimble use of every available medium to carry her vision of domestic utopia to
an ever-larger mass audience. ¶ In a postindustrial America of two-job households, long work hours,
longer commutes, and hectic schedules, Stewart's designs for living—home-baked breads, hand-painted
napkin rings, lovingly refurbished chairs—tap into a deep-seated yearning for a gracious way of life
centered around hearth and family. If a majority of her readers lack the initiative to prepare an Easter
ham, as Stewart once prescribed, in a pan lined with "tender, young, organically grown grass," no matter.
For her millions of fans, it is comfort enough to glimpse Stewart's vision and to know that they *could*
achieve it—when and if they ever found the time (a much more important commodity than money in
the Stewart scheme of things). ¶ Reared in a working-class New Jersey town, Stewart pursued the
American dream first at Barnard College, where her blond good looks enabled her to moonlight as a
model, then on Wall Street. In the early 1980s, inspired by her own renovation of a fixer-upper house
she and her then-husband had bought in Connecticut, she chucked her handsome stockbroker's salary
for the riskier venture of style arbitration. The runaway success of her first lavishly illustrated dream
book, *Entertaining* (1982), brought home an eternal verity: Lots of people want to be told how to live.
This truth had long been recognized by others, but Stewart was the first to turn her knowledge into a
media empire that fairly defined the buzzword "synergy": a trend-setting magazine, a syndicated
newspaper column, a string of best-selling books, a syndicated television show, a regular "Ask Martha"
radio feature, a Web site, a mail-order business, and lucrative product lines for the mass-market discount
store Kmart. ¶ For Martha Stewart, the self-described workaholic and entrepreneur, media saturation
translates into a very good thing, indeed: an estimated personal worth of $250 to $300 million, and for
Martha Stewart Living Omnimedia, the company she created after buying out her interests in Time,
Inc., in early 1997, an estimated $20 to $25 million in annual profits on revenues of $120 million in its
first year of operation. More bluntly than Stewart's fanciful domestic ministrations, those bottom-line
figures express another old-fashioned message: If you work hard enough, you can have it all.

1954— PHIL DONAHUE MAY HAVE PIONEERED THE QUASI-TABLOID, PARTICIPATORY FORMAT OF THE MODERN DAYTIME TALK SHOW—ONE PART JOURNALISTIC INQUIRY, TWO PARTS PRURIENCE— BUT OPRAH WINFREY PERFECTED IT. SHE HAS TURNED AN HOUR OF MIDDAY CHAT INTO THE ILLUSION OF AN intimate heart-to-heart with millions of anonymous viewers. ¶ What made Oprah, as the warm and forthright star came to be known by almost everyone, different from other hosts was her willingness to bare her own soul and her uncanny ability to relate to the problems of her guests, and they to hers. Using the now-legendary events of her own troubled life—a childhood of poverty in the racist South, rape by a cousin when she was 9, pregnancy as a teenager, and a chronic, operatic struggle with her weight—as a springboard, Winfrey turned her show into a nonthreatening forum for exploring both the ordinary problems of ordinary women (with weight, with commitment-phobic men, with recalcitrant husbands), as well as such once-taboo subjects as incest, domestic abuse, and homosexuality. Possessing what *Time* magazine called "a direct pipeline to the nation's psyche," Winfrey changed what America talked about in public. ¶ Then, at some point in the ever-upward trajectory of her career, Winfrey passed from being America's favorite girlfriend to becoming a national tastemaker. The phenomenal power her personal convictions carry is truly unparalleled. The books she likes shoot to the top of the bestseller lists. Musicians she invites on her show watch their records climb the charts. Diets concocted by her personal cook influence the eating habits of millions. ¶ Launched nationally in 1986, *The Oprah Winfrey Show* soon toppled Donahue, the reigning talk king. As her show took off, Winfrey sought new challenges. She started a film production company, took up acting (her performance in Steven Spielberg's *The Color Purple* earned her an Academy Award nomination), opened a restaurant. Meanwhile, her effort to lose weight and keep it off became something approaching a national obsession. ¶ Winfrey, whose $415 million empire makes her the wealthiest woman in show business, continues to live by the advice she once shared with *Ladies' Home Journal*. "Follow your instincts," she said. "That's where true wisdom manifests itself."

o p r a h
Winfrey

> **"**
>
> People think
> because you're
> on TV you have
> the world
> by a string.
> But I have
> struggled with
> my own self-value
> for many,
> many years.
>
> **"**

Artists &
Entertainers

"A woman who has lived many things and who sees lines and colors as an expression of living might say something that a man can't. I feel there is something unexplored about women that only a woman can explore. Men have done all they can do about it."

— Georgia O'Keeffe

Marian Anderson rehearses at the Met in New York in 1954, and (right) visits the site of her break-through 1939 concert.

1902–1993

REPEATEDLY SHUT OUT OF CONCERT HALLS IN THE COUNTRY OF HER BIRTH, THE GREAT AFRICAN-AMERICAN CONTRALTO MARIAN Anderson in 1930 went to live and tour in Europe, where audiences were more interested in her exquisite voice and technique than in the color of her skin. And yet Anderson—dignified, brave, supremely talented—never allowed the prejudices of her era to keep her down. Her cultural contribution rests as much on her warm, expansive spirit as on her arresting art. ¶ From the time she was 6 years old, a love of music guided everything that Anderson did—from scrubbing steps to earn money for a violin to joining the choir of the Union Baptist Church, her Philadelphia congregation. Early in her career, Anderson became demoralized by the professional odds stacked against her. Only the encouragement of her beloved mother convinced her to stick with it. "She didn't know a lot about singing, but she always stood behind me," she told *Ladies' Home Journal* in 1980, "even when other members of the family thought I should have found a more stable job." ¶ Anderson returned to the United States from her triumphant tour of Europe in 1935. Four years later, in the defining moment of her career, she was barred from giving a concert at Constitution Hall in Washington, D.C., by the hall's owner, the all-white Daughters of the American Revolution. An outraged First Lady Eleanor Roosevelt resigned from the D.A.R. in protest, then arranged for Anderson to sing at the Lincoln Memorial instead. The contralto's Easter Sunday concert drew 75,000 ardent supporters and millions more radio listeners. A moment of uncommon grace, the concert remains a seminal event of the American civil rights movement. Anderson broke another barrier when, at age 57, she became the first African-American to sing with New York's Metropolitan Opera. ¶ Aided by both Anderson's example and the scholarship fund she endowed, countless young African-American singers have pursued their own dreams of performing. "She was a dream maker," said one scholarship recipient, soprano Shirley Verrett. "She has cast a shadow that embraces us all."

marian
Anderson

I had gone to
Europe...to reach
for a place as a
serious artist,
but I never
doubted that I
must return.
I was—and am—
an American.

lucille
Ball

1911—1989

LUCILLE BALL'S FACE HAS PROBABLY BEEN SEEN BY MORE PEOPLE THAN THAT OF ANY PERSON WHO HAS EVER LIVED. THANKS TO THE WONDERS OF syndication, the great comedienne's pioneering 1950s television series, *I Love Lucy*, entertains millions daily, around the globe. ¶ Before her gift for slapstick turned *I Love Lucy* into the first hit situation comedy in television history (thereby solidifying the sitcom as a genre), the gorgeous redhead was a Hollywood glamour girl who never quite made it into the first tier of movie stardom. Time was running out on Ball's film career when, in 1947, she began starring in a radio comedy called *My Favorite Husband*. Asked by CBS to develop a television show with a similar premise, Ball created *I Love Lucy* as a vehicle for her and her Cuban-born husband, Desi Arnaz. (Among other motivations, she was looking for a way to keep her philandering mate, whom she'd married in 1940, close at hand.) When the show premiered as a TV series in October 1951, CBS had low expectations. It was, opined one executive, "unfunny, silly, and totally boring." Viewers had a different reaction: Embracing the show as a hilarious farce of married life, they fell in love with Lucy Ricardo, the dizzy housewife whose good-natured exploits constantly land her in hot water—from which her exasperated, but loving, bandleader husband, Ricky, must constantly extricate her. Within four months, *I Love Lucy* was the number-one show in the country. Within six months, it was being watched in some 10 million American homes (at a time when there were only 15 million working TV sets in all of America). The 1953 episode in which Lucy Ricardo delivers a baby boy—aired on the same night that Ball gave birth by C-section to her second child, Desi Arnaz, Jr.—attracted 44 million viewers, or 92 percent of the TV audience (a record yet to be surpassed). ¶ The couple was as successful at business as they were at comedy. Arnaz negotiated a contract with CBS that allowed their production company, Desilu, to keep the fees from all repeat airings of the show. That deal became the source of a vast multimillion dollar fortune that eventually made Ball one of the world's richest entertainment entrepreneurs. (After she bought out Arnaz's share of Desilu in 1960, Ball also became the first woman to head a studio by herself.) ¶ The marriage had a more dismal fate. In 1957, demoralized and exhausted by Arnaz's relentless drinking, womanizing, and gambling, Ball called off both the relationship and the series, after 179 now-classic episodes.

margaret

Bourke-White

> "
> **The camera**
>
> **is a remarkable**
>
> **instrument.**
>
> **Saturate yourself**
>
> **with your subject**
>
> **and the camera**
>
> **will all but take**
>
> **you by the hand.**
>
> "

1904-1971 THE PIONEERING PHOTOJOURNALIST MARGARET BOURKE-WHITE CREATED SOME OF THE DEFINING IMAGES OF THE 20TH CENTURY: CRACKED-EARTH DUST-BOWL FARMS, southern sharecroppers, the living dead of Buchenwald, Gandhi at his spinning wheel. ¶ Bourke-White was a staff photographer for *Fortune* magazine when, in 1934, she was propelled into a new career as a social activist. Investigating rumors of a drought out west, she was horrified to discover that the devastation stretched from the Dakotas to the Texas Panhandle. Her photographs of the disaster—dubbed the Dust Bowl—not only changed her aesthetic focus, they changed the nature of photojournalism itself. ¶ Bourke-White had turned to photography in college as a way to support herself. Her early, dramatic shots of hydroelectric dams, cityscapes, and factories captured the austere beauty of these symbols of progress. But the Dust Bowl, as she later wrote, marked "the beginning of my awareness of people in a human, sympathetic sense as subject for the camera." From then on, she used photography to drive social change. ¶ Bourke-White's lifelong affiliation with *Life* magazine started with its first issue, dated November 23, 1936. On the cover was her photograph of a massive dam being built in Montana, and inside, running across nine pages, was a series of photographs of Great Plains workers and their families. A new journalistic form was born: the photo essay. The following year, she published her groundbreaking book on southern poverty, *You Have Seen Their Faces*—a collaboration with novelist Erskine Caldwell (whom she married in 1939 and divorced three years later) and one of the era's most powerful social documents. ¶ With the outbreak of World War II, Bourke-White became a war correspondent—the first woman accredited to work in battle zones by the U.S. Armed Forces. Bourke-White stood out in this all-male profession, not least because of her striking good looks. "Generals rushed to tote her cameras," recalled fellow *Life* photographer Alfred Eisenstadt. "Even Stalin insisted on carrying her bags." ¶ Undaunted by danger and determined to get her picture at any cost, Bourke-White covered the fighting in Italy, Germany, and North Africa (where she was torpedoed) and photographed Stalin in the Kremlin in 1941 during the battle for Moscow. And she was with Lieutenant General Patton's American Third Army in 1945 when it liberated the Nazi death camps. "I implore you to believe this is true," she wrote to her *Life* editor from Buchenwald. Her searing photographs of emaciated men and women, of naked bodies piled high in ditches, made it impossible to doubt—or to forget.

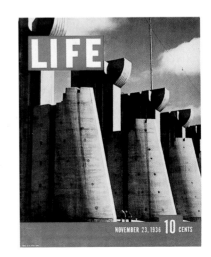

maria Callas

1923-1977

MARIA CALLAS HAD AN EXTRAORDINARY VOICE, BUT SHE WAS BY NO MEANS THE BEST SOPRANO OF HER ERA. WHY, THEN, IS SHE THE MOST ADULATED OPERA SINGER OF THE CENTURY? The answer, quite simply, is star quality. As dramatic in life as she was in the role of Puccini's *Tosca*, Callas was every inch the prima donna, a temperamental artist who could be as erratic as she was brilliant. During a performing career that spanned a mere 20 years, Callas managed to sing 43 roles and to make 22 recordings of complete operas. More importantly, she infused opera with drama, turning it into a layered *theatrical* experience, as well as a musical one. And she revived the all-but-forgotten bel canto operas of Bellini, Donizetti, and Rossini. These early 19th-century Italian operas are now central to the contemporary repertory. ¶ Even as a teenager attending Athens's National Conservatory, Callas was notable for the force and sentiment she brought to her singing. Later, of course, she became famous for her passionate musicality—as well as for her ferocious temper. She feuded with producers, canceled engagements at the last minute, stormed out of performances, broke contracts at whim. And she routinely upstaged rival divas. Difficult as she was, opera directors fought to get Callas into their concert halls: Her presence guaranteed a sellout. ¶ Her personal life was no less turbulent. The singer's only marriage—to a wealthy Italian who bankrolled her early career—ended in 1959, when she met Greek shipping magnate Aristotle Onassis, with whom she led a stormy, jet-set life that effectively halted her stage career. Onassis (who knew little about opera) refused to marry her; when he married Jacqueline Kennedy in 1968, Callas suffered a breakdown. Yet her association with Onassis never ended, and in the last years of her life, the two were said to be living together again. ¶ Callas made her last appearance in an opera in 1965 and retired altogether in 1974. Since her death in 1977, the legend has only grown. To her legions of fans, she is, as critic Will Crutchfield has written, "both the reason for and the means of learning to love opera itself."

To me the art

of music is

magnificent and

I cannot bear to

see it treated in a

shabby way.

> I would rather
>
> dance completely
>
> nude than strut
>
> in half-clothed
>
> suggestiveness,
>
> as many women
>
> do today on the
>
> streets of America.

1878—1927 AT A TIME WHEN IT WAS SCANDALOUS EVEN TO HINT THAT SOMEWHERE BENEATH A WOMAN'S PETTICOATS A BODY WAS HIDDEN, ISADORA DUNCAN DONNED A FREE-flowing translucent tunic and performed barefoot, with no stage sets. Virtually inventing modern interpretive dance—she called it the "divine expression of the human spirit through the medium of the body's movement"—Duncan shocked the recital hall audiences of America, but captivated those of Europe. In her life and art, she was the epitome of the unfettered free spirit whose fierce artistry cannot be governed by the rules and conventions to which more earthbound creatures are subject. ¶ This utterly modern woman was born in San Francisco at the height of the Victorian era. Bored by school, Duncan terminated her formal education at age 10, a decision that had the blessing of her free-spirited, musical mother. Duncan began dancing professionally at 15. At 18, she joined a New York theater company as an actress and dancer, but felt frustrated by the artificial stage conventions of the day. ¶ In 1889, Duncan, her mother, sister, and brother left America for Europe. In London, they studied Greek art at the British Museum. Soon, her performances were infused with Greek influences, including the Greek-inspired tunic that allowed audiences to see the movements of her bare

limbs. After London, she was greeted with wild enthusiasm in Paris, Berlin, and Vienna. Yet Duncan was never appreciated in her native country, which found her lewd. ¶ Duncan's emancipation on stage was matched in her personal life. An outspoken proponent of free love, she had myriad affairs and bore two children (who died in a tragic 1913 accident) by two different fathers, neither of whom she married. ¶ Duncan's life ended freakishly when her neck was snapped as the long scarf she was wearing became entangled in the spoked rear wheel of a roadster she had just boarded. Seconds earlier, she had waved goodbye to friends, saying, "I am going to my glory." Indeed, her glory is the vibrant tradition of modern dance.

isadora

Duncan

ella
Fitzgerald

"

> I thought my
> singing was pretty
> much hollering,
> but a bandleader
> named Chick
> Webb didn't.
>
> "

1917—1996 "SHE WAS THE LADY WHO TAUGHT US ALL HOW TO SING," SINGER TONY BENNETT SAID OF ELLA FITZGERALD. MORE TO THE POINT, SILVERY-VOICED FITZGERALD TAUGHT US HOW TO LISTEN. ¶ DURING A SIX-DECADE CAREER, SHE RELEASED SOME 250 albums, covering everything from swing music to bebop jazz to country and western. But it was the series of "songbook" albums, produced by impresario Norman Granz and recorded on the Verve label, that stands as her greatest accomplishment. Beginning with *Ella Fitzgerald Sings the Cole Porter Songbook* in 1956, Fitzgerald and Granz dusted off both the better- and lesser-known tunes of America's top songwriters—Rodgers and Hart, Duke Ellington, Irving Berlin, George and Ira Gershwin (in a peerless 53-song, 5-LP set), Harold Arlen, Jerome Kern, Johnny Mercer—and revealed for the first time their

depth and inherent genius. "I never knew how good our songs were," gushed Ira Gershwin, "until I heard Ella Fitzgerald sing them." ¶ As a girl, Fitzgerald dreamed of becoming a dancer and occasionally performed for change on street corners in her hometown of Yonkers, New York. In 1934, she entered an amateur talent contest at Harlem's famed Apollo Theater, intending to dance. Instead, the tall, gawky teenager, paralyzed by stage fright, began singing in desperation. As the last clear note diminished, the packed house went wild. Fitzgerald pocketed the $25 first prize and went on to become the "canary" for Harlem bandleader Chick Webb's swing orchestra. ¶ A workhorse who performed constantly, Fitzgerald toured until 1993, when poor health finally stopped her. Fans adored her tonal purity, clear articulation, unfailing buoyancy (Fitzgerald could always be counted on to swing), and, above all, her ability to "scat." She'd begun improvising these nonsense syllables back in 1945, and they became her signature. Other vocalists sang scat, but none with the clarity, timing, or sheer inventiveness of the incomparable Ella.

ANE FONDA'S ORKOUT BOOK

by Jane Fonda
with photographs
by Steve Schapiro

1937—

NOVELIST F. SCOTT FITZGERALD FAMOUSLY OBSERVED THAT THERE ARE NO SECOND ACTS IN AMERICAN LIFE. ACTRESS, ACTIVIST, ENTREPRENEUR, JANE FONDA HAS PROVEN THAT A SUFFICIENTLY enterprising woman can enjoy not only a second act, but a third and a fourth as well. Each of Fonda's many incarnations has uniquely reflected its era— purring sex-kitten in the early 1960s, strident 1970s antiwar activist, 1980s aerobics coach, consummate corporate wife in the 1990s—but it was her role as workout guru that left the deepest imprint on popular culture. Fonda helped popularize the idea of fitness for a mass audience. She became America's personal trainer. ¶ When *The Jane Fonda Workout Book* appeared in 1981, few Americans belonged to health clubs. Working out was something professional (male) athletes did. But after the excesses of the 1960s and '70s, health consciousness was rising and Americans wanted to get fit. Fonda's step-by-step regimen became a huge bestseller—and the cornerstone of a mini-empire of fitness clubs, music cassettes to work out by, and a video that smashed all known sales records. ¶ Fonda, the daughter of revered actor Henry Fonda, grew up unhappy in Hollywood. Her father was emotionally distant and her mother committed suicide when she was 12 (a fact she learned from an indiscreet boarding-school classmate). She made her first feature film in 1960. Eight years later, she emerged as an international sexpot in *Barbarella*, directed by her first husband, Roger Vadim. Then, in one of her periodic personal transformations, Fonda became active in protesting the Vietnam War, earning infamy as "Hanoi Jane" by posing at the controls of a North Vietnamese anti-aircraft gun. She also left playboy Vadim for left-wing radical Tom Hayden and won critical praise (and two Oscars) for such films as *Klute* (1971) and *Coming Home* (1978). ¶ In 1991, two years after divorcing Hayden, Fonda tackled what some called her most surprising role yet: wife of billionaire media baron Ted Turner. Embracing this new part with her usual gusto, Fonda professed greater happiness than at any other time during her varied all-American career.

You can do one of two things; just shut up, which is something I don't find easy, or learn an awful lot very fast, which is what I tried to do.

j a n e

Fonda

greta

Garbo

> 66
>
> **I had made**
>
> **enough faces.**
>
> 99
>
> *[on why
> she retired]*

OF ALL THE GREAT ICONS OF HOLLYWOOD'S GOLDEN AGE, GRETA GARBO PRODUCED PERHAPS THE SLIMMEST BODY OF WORK. BETWEEN 1924 AND 1941, THE SULTRY SWEDISH ACTRESS APPEARED IN A TOTAL OF 28 MOVIES—14 SILENT FILMS AND 14 TALKIES. THEN she took a short break that kept getting longer: a year, 5 years, 10 years, forever. Always a private person, Garbo at age 36 simply walked away from Hollywood and into a solitude of her own making. ¶ Garbo—born Greta Gustafsson to poor parents in Stockholm—worked with few truly outstanding directors during her truncated career. She never won an Oscar (though in 1954 the Academy presented her with a Lifetime Achievement Award). Yet many critics consider her the finest actress in movie history because she had an unerring intuition for doing the right thing in front of a camera. She was also the first movie star to appeal equally to both sexes. ¶ In films like *Anna Christie* (1930), the talking picture in which Garbo's deep, seductive, heavily accented English was first heard; *Grand Hotel* (1932), in which she uttered her trademark line, "I want to be alone"; and *Ninotchka* (1939), the Ernst Lubitsch comedy in which "Garbo laughs," the enigmatic star projected an almost hypnotic intensity. Fervid, romantic, a hair's breadth this side of melodrama, her acting was of a style all her own—a fact that perhaps explains why she never spawned any serious imitators. ¶ "What, when drunk, one sees in other women," the critic Kenneth Tynan observed, "one sees in Garbo sober." Her severe Scandinavian beauty attracted men and women alike. And though she hated crowds, Garbo loved company of her own choosing: She had affairs with John Gilbert, the sexiest leading man of the 1920s; conductor Leopold Stokowski; bisexual British photographer Cecil Beaton; and aristocratic Cuban socialite Mercedes de Acosta. ¶ But if Garbo seduced, she remained beyond reach herself. She never married, never had children—didn't do much of anything at all, in fact, after 1941, when she made her last film, the comedy *Two Faced Woman*. Ingrid Bergman, cinema's other great Swedish beauty, once asked, "What can she possibly do all day?" The answer is that she kept quiet, let her early work speak for itself, and so became a kind of living ghost—less than real and yet larger than life.

"

Life today

is nervous,

sharp,

and zigzag.

That is what

I aim for in

my dances.

"

1894-1991 MARTHA GRAHAM IS THE SINGLE MOST IMPORTANT FIGURE IN THE EVOLUTION OF MODERN DANCE. IN A LONG AND active career that lasted until shortly before her death at age 96, Graham choreographed some 170 ballets, founded and directed her own vastly influential dance company, won dozens of awards (including a Presidential Medal of Freedom, the highest civilian honor bestowed by the U.S. government), and personally trained virtually every contemporary American dancer and choreographer of note. Paul Taylor, Merce Cunningham, Erich Hawkins (the Adonis-like dancer whom she briefly married in 1949, after a long and turbulent relationship), and Pearl Lang are just a few of the talents she shaped. For 60 years, Graham had one unchanging mantra: "Nothing is more revealing than movement." ¶ Graham's first great influence was the American dancer Ruth St. Denis, who, following the path blazed by Isadora Duncan, led ballet toward a more free-flowing, sensual expressiveness. Graham began studying with St. Denis in 1916. By 1930, when she formed her own company, she had abandoned the smooth prettiness of classical lyricism for a sharply angular, sexually charged aesthetic. It was an amazing leap forward—one that could not have been predicted by anything that preceded it. Indeed, many early audiences were disturbed by Graham's moody explorations of desire, guilt, rage, and sexuality. "It's not my job to look beautiful," she haughtily responded. "It's my job to look interesting." ¶ For Graham, modern dance was inextricably bound up with the emancipation of women. The female characters she created in such landmark dances as *Clytemnestra* were, she said, "every woman." Graham was also fascinated with American life and values, a preoccupation that culminated in *Appalachian Spring* (1944). This uncharacteristically warm and spirited ballet, choreographed to Aaron Copland's music, was her first big popular success, yet it too carried all the hallmarks of the Graham style: dynamic choreography; bold integration of motion, music, and stage direction; and unity of mind and body—in short, the essence of modern dance.

martha **Graham**

katharine
Hepburn

> **66**
>
> I think I was born
>
> at the right time
>
> for the thing I
>
> turned into,
>
> this new kind of
>
> modern woman
>
> who wanted to
>
> wear pants,
>
> wanted to live
>
> like a man.
>
> **99**

1907— ELEGANT, OUTSPOKEN, AND SELF-RELIANT, KATHARINE HEPBURN WAS A THOROUGHLY MODERN WOMAN WHO BROUGHT AN UNCOMPROMISING, NO-NONSENSE YANKEE SENSIBILITY—AND *SENSE*—TO BOTH HER PUBLIC AND PRIVATE ROLES. From the beginning of her career, when she stubbornly resisted the conventions of glamour for the comfort of pants, Kate the Great did things her way or not at all. (That she was an exceptional beauty with impossibly high cheekbones and a thick mane of auburn hair did not hurt.) For that spirited individualism, as well as for a seven-decade screen career that earned her 12 Oscar nominations and a record four best-actress awards, Hepburn has been an inspiring role model for several generations of women. ¶ Hepburn broke into movies in the 1930s after a mostly undistinguished stage career. On screen, she played such able women as an aviatrix in *Christopher Strong*, Jo in *Little Women*, and an understudy who becomes a star in *Morning Glory*, her first Oscar-winning role. But after teaming up with Cary Grant in 1938's *Bringing Up Baby*, a commercial disappointment that is now considered a classic "screwball comedy," Hollywood's most unconventional star was designated box-office poison.

She resuscitated her career by producing and starring in both the stage and screen versions of *The Philadelphia Story*, in which she played the imperious socialite Tracy Lord. ¶ Hepburn's collaborators include some of Hollywood's most distinguished directors and leading men. But her greatest partnership was with Spencer Tracy, with whom she made nine movies—most memorably, the smart and sexy *Adam's Rib* (1949)—and shared a 26-year love affair. Never married— Tracy, a Catholic, refused to divorce his wife—the couple remained inseparable until Tracy's death a few weeks after the completion of their last movie, 1967's *Guess Who's Coming to Dinner*. Hepburn won her second Oscar for that film, which—in one of her typically unique and personal statements of integrity—she declined ever to watch.

billie

Holiday

1915–1959

BILLIE HOLIDAY HAD MADE ONLY A HANDFUL OF RECORDINGS WHEN, IN 1935, RALPH COOPER, THE EMCEE AT HARLEM'S LEGENDARY APOLLO THEATER, HEARD HER SING. "IT AIN'T the blues," he told the club's owner. "I don't know what it is, but you got to hear her." The owner listened. Holiday was booked. She brought down the house. ¶ Cooper was right: The feelings may have been the blues, but the voice—moody, melodically inventive, and emotionally raw—was pure jazz. Today, 40 years after her premature death, Holiday remains the single most influential female vocalist in the history of American music. ¶ Born in Baltimore to a pair of unmarried teenagers, Holiday was abandoned to the care of abusive relatives by the time she was 10. It was in a brothel, where she was put to work scrubbing floors, that she first heard recordings by Louis Armstrong and the powerful blues singer Bessie Smith. After finishing fifth grade, Holiday went to New York and began picking up work in nightclubs as a nude dancer and occasional prostitute. When she finally got a chance to sing, audiences were enthralled. Beginning in the 1930s, she performed with jazz's brightest lights—Teddy Wilson, Duke Ellington, Count Basie, Artie Shaw—in the process transforming the subsidiary role of "girl singer" into an essential element of the music. ¶ Holiday's tortured personal life included poverty, abuse, rape, abandonment, and divorce, in addition to constant racial prejudice. Most calamitous of all was her chronic, unshakable addiction to heroin, which resulted in several arrests and one nine-month stint in prison. ¶ Yet, ultimately, Holiday's painful existence is inseparable from the uniqueness of her art—the bruised, haunting timbre of her voice; her languid, almost mournful, phrasing; her often heartbreaking vocal inflections. "Only somebody who'd gone through the things she did and survived," said fellow jazz vocalist Anita O'Day, "could sing from the soul the way she did."

The whole basis

for my singing

is feeling.

Unless I feel

something,

I can't sing.

1943—1970

IN THE LATE-1960S HEYDAY OF ROCK AND ROLL AS CULTURAL DEFIANCE, JANIS JOPLIN WAS THE GENRE'S FIRST FEMALE SUPERSTAR, A LARGER-THAN-LIFE FIGURE WHO POURED HER WILD SOUL INTO EVERY PERFORMANCE WITH RAUNCHY ABANDON. THE scores of female rock stars who have come after her—from Patti Smith to Courtney Love—would be inconceivable had Joplin not gotten there first. ¶ A misfit growing up in 1950s Texas ("There was nobody like me in Port Arthur," she once said), Joplin left home after high school and pursued a vagabond existence made up of cross-country hitchhiking treks, odd jobs, sex, drugs, and liquor. What distinguished her from legions of other wayfaring kids was an abiding interest in the music of such great black country blues singers as Bessie Smith and Big Mama Willie Mae Thornton. It also happened that she possessed a blues voice of her own to do her heroines proud. ¶ In 1966, Joplin lent her vocal talents to a struggling San Francisco band called Big Brother and the Holding Company, performing at that city's legendary Avalon ballroom, a command center of the burgeoning hippie movement. "I couldn't believe it, all that rhythm and power," she later said. "I had never danced when I sang, but there I was moving and jumping. I couldn't hear myself, so I sang louder and louder. By the end I was wild." ¶ The following year, Joplin appeared at the Monterey Pop Festival and stunned the

> **I'd rather not sing than sing quiet.**

huge international crowd with a passionate rendition of Mama Thornton's "Love is Like a Ball and Chain." In the best blues tradition, the song, one critic wrote, "was wrenched out of some deep dark nether region of her Texas soul." The next morning she was famous. ¶ Throughout the rest of her brief career, Joplin continued to drink excessively (she often appeared on stage swilling Southern Comfort from the bottle), inject hard drugs, and indulge in a series of torrid, if brief, affairs. Such flouting of convention secured both her legend and her premature death. She succumbed to a heroin overdose less than three weeks after the death by overdose of another rock and roll legend, Jimi Hendrix. Joplin was 27; the year, fittingly, was 1970. Her death was proof positive that the 60s were over.

janis **Joplin**

frida Kahlo

1907—1954 DURING HER SHORT AND EVENTFUL LIFETIME, MEXICAN PAINTER FRIDA KAHLO LIVED AND WORKED LARGELY IN THE SHADOW OF HER HUSBAND, REVOLUTIONARY MURALIST DIEGO RIVERA. IN THE HALF-CENTURY since her death, Kahlo has become an international heroine whose reputation is beginning to outstrip Rivera's. Her burgeoning cult is at least partly due to the perception of Kahlo as the ultimate underdog. As a bisexual, handicapped, left-wing, Latin feminist, she is the poster child for some half-dozen causes. Fortunately, her vivid, powerful paintings, most notably a series of highly symbolic self-portraits she executed in the 1930s and '40s, transcend those trendy labels. ¶ The central misfortune of Kahlo's life occurred in 1925. She was nearly killed when a streetcar struck the Mexico City bus she was riding on. Impaled on a steel railing, the 18-year-old student suffered a crushed pelvis and serious injuries to her spine and uterus. For the rest of her life she would endure excruciating physical pain as well as a heartbreaking inability to bear children. To help pass time while she recuperated, she took up painting. ¶ Kahlo met Rivera when the already legendary painter came to her school to work on murals. He praised the young woman's painting and encouraged her to become involved in the international movement. (Rivera was a devoted—but inconsistent—communist.) Their wedding in 1929 marked the beginning of one of the century's most famously tumultuous marriages. Rivera, who was 20 years Kahlo's senior, was a man of enormous appetites—for food, for experience, for sex. Kahlo was deeply wounded by his compulsive womanizing and struck back by taking numerous lovers (of both sexes) of her own, including sculptor Isamu Noguchi and exiled Russian revolutionary Leon Trotsky. Kahlo and Rivera separated periodically, and even divorced once in 1939, only to remarry a year later. ¶ Kahlo's work is often described as surrealist, but she distanced herself from those dream-obsessed artists, insisting, "I always paint my own reality." Yet her reality had elements of a nightmare. In *The Two Fridas* (1938), two images of herself sit holding hands. The heart of the figure on the right is exposed, and a severed artery spills blood into her lap; the other figure cups a small portrait of Rivera. In contrast to the public, monumental quality of her husband's work, Kahlo's paintings are intensely personal, combining her own history with that of Mexico. ¶ By the end of the 1940s Kahlo's health was deteriorating. A series of operations did little to relieve her pain, though they may have fostered a morphine dependency. Kahlo also began to drink heavily. Through it all, she remained active. She began a series of still-life paintings in 1952, and on July 2, 1954, scarcely a week before her death, she attended a protest rally with Rivera. Such bravery was typical of a woman who knew, Rivera said, "how to resist the opposing forces and triumph over them to reach a higher joy."

> I paint self-portraits because I am so often alone, because I am the person I know best.

Frida Kahlo mined her own suffering for the powerful subject matter of her compelling pictures. The Two Fridas (top left), done in 1938, is in Mexico City.

1895—1965 RARELY DOES ART INFLUENCE LIFE SO DIRECTLY AS IT DID IN 1934, WHEN DOROTHEA LANGE'S STARK DOCUMENTARY PHOTOGRAPHS OF CALIFORNIA FIELDWORKERS led the federal government to fund sanitary camps for migrants. The profound empathy with which Lange rendered her subjects gave individual human faces to the often abstract concept of the Great Depression. Then, as now, people looked at Lange's work and understood what it was to be poor and desperate, yet full of dignity. ¶ From an early age, Lange knew that photography would be her life's work. She spent many hours walking New York City's teeming streets, minutely observing the life around her. By 1918, after several apprenticeships with professional photographers, she set out to travel around the world. She got as far as San Francisco, where she established a lucrative business as a society portraitist. ¶ In the early 1930s, as global depression and drought brought new levels of misery to California, Lange turned her lens from the studio to the street. Her shots of breadlines and destitute men standing on street corners attracted the attention of economist Paul Taylor, with whom she collaborated on the study of migrant workers. In 1933, Lange divorced her husband of 15 years and married Taylor. ¶ Later, Lange ranged through the Dust Bowl states photographing careworn farmers, prematurely haggard women (most famously her *Migrant Mother* of 1936), and uprooted families. During World War II, she documented the internment of Japanese-Americans. So potent were these pictures that the government impounded many of them until after the war. ¶ Transcending photojournalism, Lange's images, observed fellow photographer Edward Steichen, "are among the most remarkable human documents ever rendered in pictures."

> **"The camera is an instrument that teaches people how to see without a camera."**

d o r o t h e a **Lange**

Madonna

> **I've been an exhibitionist since I was a very small girl. I remember always doing totally outrageous things, doing things only to shock people.**

1958—

STARTING OUT AS A DISCO SINGER OF DUBIOUS TALENT (ONE CRITIC LIKENED HER VOICE TO "MINNIE Mouse on helium"), the performer Madonna became one of the world's most celebrated entertainers. Within a decade of her first hit single, she had branched from records into videos, movies, and books, and been named "America's Smartest Business Woman" by *Forbes* magazine. Therein lay Madonna's lasting cultural significance: In an age of celebrity worship, she was a one-woman entertainment tycoon whose inimitable product, shrewdly packaged and marketed, was herself. ¶ Madonna Louise Ciccone arrived in New York City in 1978, with $37 in cash. Aided by the new medium of MTV and a keen appreciation of the power of sexual titillation, Madonna, the nascent pop singer, gained exposure through music videos as Madonna, the outrageous siren. Sporting midriff-baring thrift-store outfits, self-consciously tacky makeup, and mildly sacrilegious crucifix jewelry, she created an updated version of the old Mae West persona of unabashed, yet essentially good-natured, sexual predator. ¶ What separated Madonna from countless flashes in the pan was her ability constantly to remake herself. From trashy mid-eighties "Material Girl," as one song proclaimed, Madonna became a wife (briefly—to bad-boy screen actor Sean Penn), a gym-buffed dominatrix, a Marilyn Monroe bombshell, a Dietrichesque androgyne, and, finally, with the 1996 birth of daughter Lourdes, a doting mom. ¶ By 1997, more than 80 million Madonna albums had been sold worldwide. Meanwhile, offstage, she insured her postperformance financial health by creating film, music publishing, and recording companies. "An oddly innocent pop phenomenon harking back to the flirtatious glamour of earlier times," said one critic, "she seems likely to endure one way or another."

Monroe

m a r i l y n

> I sometimes
>
> feel as if I'm too
>
> exposed;
>
> I've given myself
>
> away, the whole of
>
> me, every part,
>
> and there's
>
> nothing left
>
> that's private,
>
> just me alone.

[1960]

1926—1962 MARILYN MONROE WAS A VICTIM OF THE HOLLYWOOD MACHINE THAT TRANSFORMED HER FROM A NAIVE, RATHER PLAIN-LOOKING BRUNETTE NAMED Norma Jean Baker into the most enduring sex goddess of all time. ¶ Born in Los Angeles to an unstable mother who was frequently institutionalized and a father she never knew, Monroe lived mostly in orphanages until she was 14, when she married for the first time. While working in an airplane factory near the end of World War II, she was discovered by an Army photographer, who got her started modeling for calendars and, later, magazines (most notoriously, the first issue of *Playboy*, in which she appeared, as she later put it, with "nothing on but the radio"). ¶ Monroe signed a contract with Twentieth Century Fox and appeared in a series of forgettable films before landing coveted roles in *The Asphalt Jungle* and *All About Eve* (both 1950). Fox launched a massive publicity campaign, and within three years, Monroe had become an icon of hilarious, dumb-blond sexuality—a part she played to perfection in such now-classic films as *Some Like It Hot* and *The Seven Year Itch*. Indeed, her overripe beauty and sheer star power are so dazzling, they threaten to obscure the fact that she was a fine, intuitive actress with impeccable comic timing. ¶ Success, however, only exacerbated Monroe's insecurity. Her high-profile marriages to powerful men—the first to baseball great Joe DiMaggio, a second to playwright Arthur Miller—ended in divorce, and her efforts to escape her studio-concocted image left her frustrated. ¶ As her dependence on narcotics escalated, Monroe's behavior became more erratic. In 1962, six weeks after being fired by Fox, she died, naked and alone, of a sleeping-pill overdose in her Los Angeles home. ¶ Today, Monroe is nearly as famous for being Marilyn Monroe— she of the impossibly tight, flesh-colored dress and breathy delivery of "Happy Birthday, Mr. President" to JFK—as she is for her film career. And in an age of conspiracy theories, she is never far from center stage, thanks to her alleged love affairs with both John Kennedy and his brother Robert, and to the sordid circumstances of her death. Yet it is onscreen, watching her trade double entendres with Tony Curtis or coo "Diamonds Are a Girl's Best Friend," that we truly see what the fuss was about. The Jayne Mansfields and Bo Dereks may come and go, but Marilyn Monroe is forever.

[Who was the real Marilyn Monroe? Entertaining the troops in Korea (left) she's at her most sensual. Her vulnerability shows strongly (below) in her last picture, The Misfits *(1961).*]

O'Keeffe

1887—1986 ASKED ONCE HOW SHE HAD DEVELOPED HER UNIQUE STYLE, ARTIST GEORGIA O'KEEFFE SAID, "I THOUGHT SOMEONE COULD TELL ME HOW TO PAINT A LANDSCAPE, but I never found that person. They could tell you how they painted their landscape, but they couldn't tell me how to paint mine." Only the greatest artists have such courage of conviction—and at the time O'Keeffe began painting, only rarely were these artists women. ¶ O'Keeffe's work—her famous sensual blowups of calla lilies and orchids, the sun-bleached cow skulls and desert landscapes—has been described as abstract, sexual, surrealist, transcendental, and mystical. Her paintings, in one critic's words, are "monumentally intimate, austerely sensual." As that paradox suggests, another label might simply be original. ¶ Raised on a Wisconsin farm, O'Keeffe knew by the age of 10 that she would be an artist. She studied at the Art Institute of Chicago, then in 1907 enrolled at New York City's Art Students' League. She was an award-winning student, but worried constantly that her work was derivative—a concern that stayed with her throughout her long career. "Before I put a brush to canvas," she said in 1930 at the peak of her powers, "I question, 'Is this mine? Is it all intrinsically of myself? Is it influenced by some idea or some photograph of an idea which I have acquired from some man?'" ¶ Early in her career, a friend sent her charcoal drawings to the photographer Alfred Stieglitz, whose famous 291 Gallery in New York exhibited the work of the avant-garde. Stieglitz was taken with the drawings, especially the fact that they had been done by a woman. (At the time, not a single American museum had a major painting by a woman artist on its walls.) So began one of the most celebrated relationships in American art. In 1917, Stieglitz, who was 24 years older than O'Keeffe, sponsored her first solo show at 291. (It was followed by 19 more.) They married in 1924. During the next 22 years, Stieglitz took some 500 photographs of O'Keeffe, making her strong face (and, in a series of famous nudes, her sinewy body) nearly as familiar as her art. ¶ From the 1930s onward, O'Keeffe spent part of each year in New Mexico, away from Stieglitz. Inspired by the desert landscape, she painted to ever-broadening recognition. In 1946, just two months before her husband's death, New York's Museum of Modern Art mounted a retrospective of her work, the first it had ever accorded a woman. ¶ O'Keeffe continued to paint, sculpt, and draw for another 40 years. From her New Mexico home, she produced a dual legacy of magnificent art and fidelity to her own special vision.

"

I feel there is

something

unexplored about

women that only

a woman can

explore.

Men have done

all they can do

about it.

"

"

I left the screen

because I didn't

want what

happened to

Chaplin

to happen to me.

When he

discarded the

little tramp,

the little tramp

turned around and

killed him.

"

PHOTOPLAY MAGAZINE November

15 Cents

Mary Pickford *Herself and Her Career*

BEGINS IN THIS ISSUE

"Beauty and Brains" Contest

Fashions and the Screen

1893–1979

MARY PICKFORD WAS THE 20TH CENTURY'S FIRST—AND BY MANY ACCOUNTS ITS SHREWDEST—FEMALE entertainment entrepreneur. The most glittering star of Hollywood's silent era, Pickford rose in a single decade from a $10-a-day bit player (in 1909) to a powerful actress-executive who commanded $250,000 a picture and exercised complete control over the scripts, direction, ownership, and distribution of her films. "It took longer to make one of Mary's contracts," complained legendary producer Samuel Goldwyn, "than it did to make one of her pictures." ¶ In 1919, realizing that the real money in film lay in distribution, Pickford, with D.W. Griffith, Charlie Chaplin, and her lover and future husband Douglas Fairbanks, founded United Artists Corporation to distribute the pictures they produced. The arrangement remains unparalleled to this day: Actors commonly form production companies to get their movies made, but no one else has ever run the company that distributes the films to theaters. ¶ A terror behind boardroom doors, Pickford was all sugar and smiles onscreen. Audiences of the magical new medium fell in love with "Little Mary," whose sweet face, framed by golden ringlets, projected a winsome appeal that made her "America's Sweetheart." Fans adored her in silent films, where she specialized in chipper, preadolescent heroines whose old-fashioned pluck saves the day. But when sound came to film, audiences had trouble accepting a grown-up, talking Mary. She retired from acting in 1933 to nurture her fortune and to live out her days at Pickfair, the lavish Hollywood mansion she acquired during her marriage to Fairbanks. ¶ In recent years, Pickford's silent-screen career has come in for some revisionist appreciation. While the scripts were sentimental, and Pickford clearly too old for her parts, her films were technically accomplished and her acting surprisingly lively and direct. In a medium made for intimacy, she established a rapport with audiences that shines through the celluloid today.

mary

Pickford

leni Riefenstahl

> **66**
>
> Whatever is
>
> purely realistic,
>
> slice-of-life,
>
> what is average,
>
> quotidian, doesn't
>
> interest me.
>
> Only the unusual,
>
> the specific,
>
> excites me.
>
> **99**

1902— IF PROPAGANDA IS THE CENTURY'S CONSUMMATE ART FORM, THEN LENI RIEFENSTAHL MUST BE CONSIDERED ONE OF ITS MOST INFLUENTIAL ARTISTS. FILMMAKER TO THE NAZIS, RIEFENSTAHL MYTHOLOGIZED FASCIST POMP AND pageantry in *Triumph of the Will*, a chilling record of the 1934 Nazi Party Congress at Nuremberg. Cinema scholars still cite the documentary as the greatest piece of pure political propaganda ever made. Certainly its images—endless parades of jackbooted Nazis, a stadium filled with 100,000 heiling Hitlerites, the fuhrer himself maniacally rolling his eyes as he addresses his assembled minions—remain burned in the memories of all who have seen them. ¶ Athletic, graceful, and ravishingly beautiful, the Berlin-born Riefenstahl launched her film career as an actress, but soon turned to directing. Her mystical, dramatically lit 1932 film, *The Blue Light*, caught the eye of Adolf Hitler, who proposed that the young director make a movie about his godlike rule over Germany's Nazi party. *Triumph of the Will* won critical accolades for its skillful editing and innovative camera angles. So did Riefenstahl's next documentary, *Olympia*, a

stunning two-part record of the 1936 Olympic Games in Berlin that has been called the greatest sports movie ever made. ¶ Accused of being a Nazi collaborationist, Riefenstahl always claimed she was an apolitical artist whose only crime was naiveté. (The defense is somewhat disingenuous: She enjoyed a relationship with Hitler so close that they were rumored to be lovers.) She was arrested by Allied forces during the fall of Germany, but eventually exonerated of Nazi war crimes. "I wish I never made the damn film," Riefenstahl has said of *Triumph of the Will*. That sentiment is shared by the many film buffs who love her artistry but despise her subject matter.

Athletes

"As soon as the racket was in my hand, I knew that this sport was going to be my sport, and that I was going to do everything I could to be the best the world had seen. Before too many volleys had passed over the net, I knew one other thing, too—that I was going to make sure everybody, regardless of class, color, or gender, got a chance to play this wonderful sport."

—Billie Jean King

nadia Comaneci

THE IDEA OF PERFECTION IN ATHLETICS WAS MOSTLY THEORETICAL—UNTIL NADIA COMANECI SHOWED UP AT THE 1976 OLYMPIC GAMES IN MONTREAL. PERFORMING ON THE UNEVEN BARS ON THE GAMES' OPENING DAY, THE SOLEMN, DARK-EYED ROMANIAN GYMNAST, WHO AT AGE 14 STOOD 4' 10" AND WEIGHED 86 pounds, received a judges' mark of 10.00—the first such score ever awarded in Olympic competition. By the time the prodigy finished her assault on the record books, she had won three gold medals and six additional "perfect 10s." ¶ In unseating beloved Russian Olympic champ Olga Korbut, the pigtailed darling of the 1972 Munich Games, Comaneci set new standards of technical mastery. Her performances incorporated moves that no gymnast had ever before attempted—dangerous, high-flying twists and somersaults executed with an almost preternatural calm. After Comaneci, the sport became much more dangerous—and incredibly popular. Enthralled by Comaneci's unearthly contortions, preadolescent girls all over the world began flocking to gymnastics classes. And Comaneci became an overnight celebrity. "She is the most famous of all Romanians," remarked one expatriate, adding "probably not even Dracula was as famous." ¶

At the 1980 Olympics, Comaneci, 5 inches taller and 20 pounds heavier, won two gold and two silver medals. By then she was partaking fully of the perks of celebrity Romanian style. But after her former coach Bela Karolyi defected to the United States, Comaneci found her every move monitored by Romania's omnipresent secret police. ¶ In 1989—just days before dictator Nicolae Ceausescu was toppled in a bloody revolt—Comaneci slipped out of Romania in the middle of the night and escaped to the United States. Eventually, she fell in love with Bart Conner, a fellow gymnast and two-time American gold-medal winner. In 1996, she returned to Romania, where she married Conner in Bucharest's ancient Romanian Orthodox Casin Monastery.

"

I was very happy

to score the

first perfect score

in Olympic history,

but I have

already scored 19

perfect scores

before the

Olympics so

I wasn't very

excited.

"

babe **Didrikson**

> It's not enough just to swing at the ball. You've got to loosen your girdle and really let her fly.

1914—1956 BABE DIDRIKSON ZAHARIAS WAS NOT ONLY THE 20TH CENTURY'S GREATEST FEMALE ATHLETE, SHE WAS possibly its greatest athlete, period. She set more records and won more medals and tournaments than any other athlete of her era, male or female. ¶ "My goal," she recalled in her autobiography, "was to be the greatest athlete that ever lived." She played hard, played to win, and made no apologies for either her competitiveness or her skills, which were Promethean. And she did it at a time—the 1930s, 40s, and 50s—when women were viewed as skeptically on fields of play as they were in corporate boardooms. ¶ Mildred Ella Didrikson showed extraordinary athletic prowess from the moment she began playing sandlot baseball in her hometown of Beaumont, Texas. Her nickname "Babe" was a nod to the reigning king of baseball, Babe Ruth. Later, when she played on a semipro women's basketball team, she was dubbed "the Texas Tornado." ¶ Endowed with a stunning versatility, Didrikson was proficient in every sport she tried, and excelled at most, including basketball, diving, tennis, track and field, and golf. In 1932, she became a national sensation after winning five of the eight events she entered at the National Amateur Athletic Union track and field championships. Her overall score was more than double that of the next closest *team*. ¶ At the Olympics in Los Angeles that same summer, Didrikson was restricted to three events. She set world records, winning gold medals in the javelin and 80-meter hurdles. She would have won the gold in the high jump as well, except that the judges objected to her controversial technique of hurling herself head first over the pole. She was awarded the silver instead. ¶ Ridiculed in the media for her "mannish" looks and dismissed as a "muscle moll," Didrikson was subjected to endless speculation about her sexual identity. The speculation quieted down somewhat after she married retired wrestler George Zaharias in 1938. (Didrikson was never an open lesbian, but a golfer named Betty Dodd was almost certainly her great love.) ¶ Around the time of her marriage, Didrikson discovered golf. In 1947, she won 17 straight amateur tournaments, setting a record that remains unsurpassed to this day by a golfer of either sex. Also that year, she helped found the Ladies Professional Golf Association, still the country's largest sports organization for women, largely to ensure that there would be enough pro tournaments, with large enough purses, for her to prosper as a professional. Her desire to earn a living as an athlete drew reproaches from the media, but she went on to become the first female athlete ever to earn more than $100,000 a year.

gertrude
Ederle

> **I just knew if
> it could be done,
> it had to be done,
> and I did it.**

THE WHOLE WORLD SEEMED MAD FOR SPORTS IN THE 1920S, SPORTS AND THE LARGER-THAN-LIFE HEROES THEY produced—Babe Ruth swatting home runs for the Yankees, Bobby Jones and Babe Didrikson tearing up golf's fairways, Big Bill Tilden and sexy Suzanne Lenglen transforming the game of tennis. Of all the decade's stars, however, none outshone Gertrude Ederle. After swimming across the English Channel in 1926, Ederle became the most celebrated athlete on earth, male or female. ¶ The gray Channel was the Everest of long-distance swimmers, 21 miles of dangerous currents, nasty weather, and hypothermia-inducing cold. Intrepid (some would say foolhardy) swimmers had been trying to cross it for more than a century by the time Ederle came on the scene. Only five (male) athletes had ever made it, and conventional wisdom held that a woman could never succeed. "Even the most uncompromising champion of the rights and capacities of women must admit that in contests of physical skill, speed, and endurance they must remain forever the weaker sex," the *London Daily News* editorialized on the very day 19-year-old Ederle waded into the water at Cape Gris-Nez, France. ¶ A jazz-loving, thoroughly modern American girl, "plucky" Trudy Ederle had impeccable athletic credentials: Winner of three medals at the 1924 Paris Olympics, she held 18 different world records. ¶ "Gee, but it's cold," was Ederle's only comment as she entered the water shortly after 7 a.m. Fourteen hours and 30 minutes later she walked out of the water at Kingsdown, cheered by thousands who had burned bonfires to light her way. Not only had Ederle become the first woman to swim the Channel, she had shaved nearly two hours off the record. Back in New York, the "Queen of the Waves" was feted with the largest ticker-tape parade in the city's history. Fame exacted a stiff price. She lost much of the hearing in one ear during her swim and remained partially deaf for the rest of her life. ¶ Ederle recoiled from the spotlight, but her famous feat took on a life of its own. Inspired by her example, millions of women took up swimming (during the 20s, some 60,000 earned American Red Cross certificates). The sport remains one of the top recreational pursuits of American women.

"
Not many people

can spend their

lives doing

what they like

to do best.

I happen to be

one of those few

who can.

"

1912—1969 THE IMMENSE POPULARITY OF WOMEN'S FIGURE SKATING, AMERICA'S SECOND MOST-WATCHED SPORT ON TELEVISION, CAN BE TRACED ALMOST DIRECTLY TO SONJA HENIE. AN OLYMPIC MEDALIST, 10-TIME WORLD CHAMPION, AND Hollywood idol, Henie was to skating what Babe Ruth was to baseball: a larger-than-life performer whose exploits forever changed the way athletes performed—and the way fans responded. ¶ Daughter of a Norwegian furrier, Henie skated in her first Winter Olympics at the age of 11. She didn't win a medal, but left a lasting mark by competing in a knee-length flared skirt that would have been considered risqué on an adult. Four years later, in 1928, her rivals all sported elegant Henie-inspired costumes, but they couldn't compete with the golden girl's athletic leaps and twists. She won the first of a record three consecutive Olympic gold medals. ¶ A student of ballet, the "Pavlova of the Ice" introduced the now-standard elements of dance and showmanship (blond and glamorous, she smiled at all costs) into what had been a stiff, almost perfunctory sport in which competitors lurched through a repertory of compulsory exercises, seldom bothering to link one move to the next. Her other innovations were myriad: She popularized white skate boots, executed jumps previously

attempted only by men, performed sold-out public exhibitions in the off-season, traded on fame to become a corporate spokesperson, and made a smooth transition to Hollywood stardom once her amateur skating days ended. ¶ Less original was her legendary self-absorption. A temperamental princess who favored mink and oversized diamonds, Henie demanded star treatment from judges, fellow skaters, and her adoring public. At the 1936 Olympics in Germany (her last), she committed a greater offense: Finishing her program, she shouted "Heil, Hitler" and raised her arm to the watching führer. A friendship ensued, with Hitler entertaining the skater on several occasions at his Bavarian headquarters. ¶ Henie was criticized for cavorting with Nazis, but wartime infamy did nothing to dull the admiration of her fans. Beginning in 1936, the star appeared in 11 Hollywood movies in 12 years, becoming one of the biggest box-office draws in America.

s o n j a
Henie

"

Be bold.
If you're going to
make an error,
make a doozy,
and don't be afraid
to hit the ball.

"

billie jean King

BILLIE JEAN MOFFITT—A.K.A. "LITTLE MISS MOFFITT," AS THE PRESS DUBBED HER—FIRST BURST ONTO THE TENNIS scene in 1961, capturing her first Wimbledon doubles title at age 17. By the time Billie Jean King (she married college classmate Larry King in 1965) retired from active play in the late 1980s, she had dominated women's tennis for nearly 25 years, winning more titles than any player of her era, including 20 at Wimbledon. ¶ King became the archetype of the scrappy, passionate, utterly aggressive contemporary female athlete—one who made women's tennis as exciting to watch as men's and fought for prize monies that reflected that equity. In 1973, when she famously squared off against 55-year-old former men's Wimbledon champ Bobby Riggs in a $100,000 winner-takes-all "Battle of the Sexes," she was—despite such long-standing handicaps as bad eyesight, difficulties with breathing, and "chubby little legs" that gave her chronic knee pain—indisputably one of the greatest female players in history. ¶ King took

umbrage at Riggs's boast that even the most extraordinary female player could not beat a reasonably fit man in a sporting competition and challenged him to a match. A raucous crowd of 30,472—the largest ever for a tennis event—gathered at the Houston Astrodome to watch. They, and 50 million television viewers, witnessed a rout: a straight-set, 6-4, 6-3, 6-3, victory for the bespectacled 29-year-old woman. Riggs was rendered a historical footnote. King went on to do more than any other single person to advance the cause of women in sports. ¶ Despite her impressive string of titles, her most lasting achievements may have come outside the lines. In addition to fighting for equal money for women, she cofounded and presided over the Women's Tennis Association, a players' union; was the first woman athlete to be named "Sportsperson of the Year" by *Sports Illustrated*; cofounded the first sports magazine for women, *WomenSports*; and with her husband, established a chain of tennis camps and proshops. ¶ A palimony suit brought by a female ex-lover in 1981 pushed her toward an admission of bisexuality, but did not appreciably diminish the respect she commanded. Combining athletic talent and business savvy, King paved the way for every woman athlete-entrepreneur who has followed.

suzanne
Lenglen

1899—1938 THE MODERN ERA OF WOMEN'S TENNIS WAS BORN IN 1919, WHEN 20-YEAR-OLD SUZANNE LENGLEN CROSSED THE CHANNEL FROM HER NATIVE France to compete in the All-England championships at Wimbledon. After easily dispatching the players in her draw, Lenglen met Mrs. Lambert Chambers, grand dame of British tennis, in the tournament final. Most aficionados considered Chambers unbeatable. Lenglen had other ideas. In three grueling sets, she prevailed 10-8, 4-6, 9-7. Along the way, she charmed the capacity crowds with her skimpy outfits, balletic leaps, and mortally accurate groundstrokes. With this victory, Lenglen took a polite ladies' lawn game and turned it into a fiercely competitive sport closely resembling the women's tennis played today.

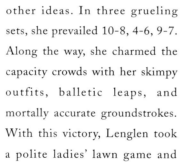

> *Some seem to believe I am tied up hands and feet by becoming a professional. To me it is an escape from bondage and slavery.*

¶ Lenglen was the greatest player of her day—an assessment shared even by her closest rival, the American tennis great Helen Wills. During a career cut short by pernicious anemia, Lenglen was a six-time champion of both Wimbledon and the French Open. Not only did she play hard, chasing down every ball and drilling shots past overmatched opponents, she practiced hard—hours a day even as a child. In her prime, Lenglen dropped just a single match. ¶ Like many a modern tennis player, the temperamental Lenglen was driven by parents whose shared ambition was to ride their daughter's talent to wealth and glory. (Hers were the original obnoxious tennis mom and dad.) The effect on Lenglen was telling. In addition to her operatic outbursts, she was prone to depression and nervous attacks. She went professional in 1926, signing a lucrative contract that paid her to play in exhibition matches rather than enter tournaments (then limited to amateurs). But ambitious parents or no, Lenglen would doubtless have played for the sheer glory of the game. Therein lies her great contribution: By playing hard and playing for keeps, she demonstrated that women loved to win just as much as men did.

GOING INTO THE FINAL LAP OF THE 4X100 RELAY AT THE 1960 ROME OLYMPICS, THE U.S. WOMEN'S TEAM WAS IN DEEP TROUBLE: AN ERRANT BATON PASS HAD LEFT AMERICAN SPRINTER WILMA RUDOLPH TWO STRIDES OFF THE LEAD. IN THE LIGHTNING-FAST WORLD OF INTERNATIONAL track and field, where two seconds can mean the difference between first place and last, the deficit seemed insurmountable. Four years earlier, the team had earned a bronze medal in the 400-meter relay with Rudolph running anchor; now it would take a miracle for them to get the gold they had come to Rome to win. ¶ Head back, long legs churning fluidly, the 6-foot-tall Rudolph set off in pursuit. With an appreciative Roman crowd roaring "La Gazelle," Rudolph overtook the lead, then breezed to the finish three full steps ahead of her nearest rival. In leading the United States to this dramatic come-from-behind victory, Rudolph earned her third gold medal of the Rome Olympics, a first for an American woman.¶ Rudolph, said Olympic historian Bud Greenspan, "was the Jesse Owens of women's track and field, and, like Jesse, she changed the sport for all time." In addition to being, in Greenspan's words, a "benchmark for little black girls to aspire to" (Jackie Joyner-Kersee, Florence Griffith Joyner, and Gail Devers have all acknowledged Rudolph as a role model), she made track and field more appealing to all girls—not least because her statuesque good looks and abundant social grace helped redefine notions of femininity in athletics. Rudolph proved, as William C. Rhoden wrote in *The New York Times*, that a woman "could be tall and lithe with the good looks associated with fashion and still run with a vengeance."

> "
> When I was
> running,
> I had the sense of
> freedom,
> of running in
> the wind...
> When I ran,
> I felt like
> a butterfly.
> "

w i l m a

Rudolph

Pioneers & Adventurers

"Please know that I am quite aware of the hazards. I want to do it because I want to do it. Women must try to do things as men have tried. When they fail, their failure must be but a challenge to others."

—Amelia Earhart
(in a letter to her husband before her last flight)

66

When I first approached corporate CEOs—both men and women—they all blushed at the word 'breast.' Most people didn't understand how devastating breast cancer is socially, culturally, emotionally, and, especially, physically.

99

1946- IN 1980, NANCY GOODMAN BRINKER WATCHED HELPLESSLY AS HER BELOVED OLDER SISTER, SUSAN KOMEN, SUCCUMBED TO THE RAVAGES OF METASTATIC BREAST CANCER. SINCE CHILDHOOD EACH SISTER had been the other's closest friend and confidante. So Brinker might have been forgiven if she had simply wallowed in depression or raged at the injustice of a world in which a vibrant, 36-year-old wife and mother could find herself the helpless hostage of such a devastating disease. Instead, she took action. ¶ Two years later, armed with just $200 and a shoebox full of names to contact, Brinker launched the Susan G. Komen Foundation, named in honor of her sister and dedicated to a single mission: to eradicate breast cancer as a life-threatening disease. ¶ Today, the Komen Foundation's mission remains unchanged, but its size and scope have been transformed—as has the public's awareness of the disease. The country's largest private funder of research dedicated solely to breast cancer, the foundation by 1998 raised more than $90 million, awarded more than 800 grants, and had pioneered such innovative fund-raising strategies as Race for the Cure, a 5K fitness run/walk held annually in dozens of cities around the world. Herself a breast-cancer survivor, Brinker has become the country's most prominent advocate for research, education, screening, and treatment for this still-baffling disease, which continues to claim the lives of 44,000 American women a year.

n a n c y

Brinker

helen gurley
Brown

1922—

IN THE PRE-DAWN OF THE SEXUAL REVOLUTION, AN ADVERTISING COPYWRITER NAMED HELEN GURLEY BROWN DARED TO defend an unmarried woman's right to have satisfying physical relationships—even with married men. In her controversial 1962 bestseller *Sex and the Single Girl* and, beginning three years later, as the neophyte editor of *Cosmopolitan* magazine, Brown used her editorial bully pulpit to demolish the 1950s-style cultural double-standard that said premarital sex was fine for red-blooded boys, but good girls didn't do it until they were married. ¶ Brown was encouraged to write *Sex and the Single Girl* by her husband, magazine-executive-turned-Hollywood-producer David Brown, after he heard about her adventures as a single working girl in the 1940s and 50s. It was likewise David Brown who had the idea of taking *Cosmopolitan*, a cash-bleeding albatross, and turning it into a clearinghouse for frank talk on sex, work, love...and sex. After winning the editor's job, Brown put a buxom blond on the cover of her first issue, in July 1965; next to the sexy picture ran the lines (written, as would the cover lines for the next 31 years, by her husband), "World's Greatest Lover—What it was like to be wooed by him." ¶ Over the years, cleavage on the cover and articles that promised to teach women how to snare men would become an internationally recognized *Cosmo* staple. The remade magazine took off, eventually achieving a peak monthly circulation of nearly 3 million. Meanwhile, the idealized woman it was written for became celebrated as "that Cosmo girl"—a distinctively modern woman who worked hard to improve herself and found it liberating to be thought of as a sex object. When Brown retired as *Cosmo*'s editor in 1996, as a publishing legend, newsstands everywhere were crowded with magazines trumpeting the same basic message.

I have no compunction about saying that sex is pleasurable and the man-woman relationship is the most exciting, dramatic thing in the world.

THEY CALLED HER THE PEOPLE'S PRINCESS, NOT JUST FOR HER REMARKABLE COMPASSION FOR AIDS patients, sick children, and victims of land mines, but also because her fairy-tale life kept veering from the script in a way ordinary folks could relate to. The eating disorders, the adulterous husband, the overbearing in-laws, the embarrassing divorce: These things happened to regular people, not to princesses. It was as if Diana had gone to the ball only to discover the slipper didn't fit after all. ¶ Willowy, flaxen-haired Lady Diana Spencer married His Highness Charles Philip Arthur George, Prince of Wales, in July 1981. Thus was launched one of the more extraordinary romances of modern times. Not between Charles and Di—the remote 32-year-old future king and his girlish 19-year-old bride (and distant cousin) were an ill-matched pair from the start—but between Diana and an adoring public. Because she was beautiful, because she introduced a measure of vivacity to Britain's stuffy royal family, because she bore an "heir and a spare" to the throne of all England, because she hobnobbed with movie stars and recording artists, because she came to realize that her enormous celebrity provided a unique opportunity to do charitable work, Diana became the most photographed—and most idolized—woman on earth. ¶ In Diana's mass popularity, of course, lay the roots of her untimely death: She was killed in a 1997 car wreck in Paris as a drunken chauffeur tried to outrace paparazzi intent on snapping pictures of her and her Egyptian playboy beau. The world had watched Diana grow from coltish bride to elegant woman. Now it watched as she was too soon laid to rest. In London, millions of mourners—ordinarily stiff-upper-lipped Britons awash in tears—lined the cortege route from St. James's Palace to Westminster Abbey, where dignitaries from around the world paid respects and her old chum, singer Elton John, crooned a sad farewell. More than a billion others watched the stirring spectacle on TV as the funeral was beamed live around the world. ¶ One of the 20th century's most scintillating figures in life, Diana in death became something greater—a symbol of a flawed life creatively lived for the short time it lasted.

> "One minute
> I was a nobody,
> the next minute
> I was the Princess
> of Wales."

[*Diana was increasingly known for her compassion and humanitarian work. Here (in 1994) she comforts an 11-year-old Angolan girl who lost a leg during an air raid.*]

Diana

princess of wales

amelia
Earhart

> **There really is not anything amazing in liking to fly. The amazing thing is that so few women, seeing what sport men are having in the air, are doing it themselves.**

1897—1937 FOR AMELIA EARHART, IT WAS LOVE AT FIRST FLIGHT. FROM THE MOMENT THE KANSAS NATIVE TOOK HER FIRST RIDE IN AN AIRPLANE IN 1919 SHE WAS HOOKED. WITHIN A year, she was taking flying lessons. ¶ In 1928, when publisher George Putnam began looking for "an American girl of the right image" to make a transatlantic flight over the same route followed in 1927 by Charles Lindbergh, Earhart, by then a social worker in Boston, was the chosen one. Although she was just a passenger, the flight brought her instant fame. In an era of public infatuation with air travel, the very idea that a *woman* was having such an adventure was almost unimaginably exotic. (Earhart ended up marrying Putnam in the bargain.) ¶ In 1932, Earhart was alone in the cockpit when she flew her own plane across the Atlantic, becoming the first woman ever to do so and setting a record for speed as well. Five years and a dazzling array of "firsts" later, the "Lady Lindy" of aviation's golden age disappeared—lost and presumed dead in the middle of an island-hopping attempt to circumnavigate the globe. ¶ With her tousled short hair, affinity for men's tailored clothing, and no-nonsense manner, Earhart stands with the young Katharine Hepburn as one of the great androgynous heroines of the period between the two world wars. Her airborne feats dared millions of less liberated admirers to believe in a fundamental truth: Anything men could do, women could do, too—as well or better. She eagerly spread that gospel as she crisscrossed America in her plane, giving lectures and demonstrating her aviation skills to worshipful crowds. ¶ Earhart had the uncanny ability of making her dangerous work look easy. But her last journey, which at 29,000 miles was to have been the longest ever made, proved too ambitious even for her. She and her navigator were on the final leg of the trip when, on July 2, 1937, their twin-engine Lockheed Electra simply disappeared. ¶ In Earhart's magnificent success and her equally spectacular failure over the Pacific lie the twin components of her legacy: a bold desire to lead women into exclusively male domains, coupled with a willingness to pay any price for the privilege.

> **"**
>
> I got a lot
> of credit for having
> gone public with
> my mastectomy,
> but if I hadn't
> been the wife of
> the President of
> the United States,
> the press would
> not have come
> racing after my
> story, so in a way
> it was fate.
>
> **"**

1918—

ALTHOUGH BETTY FORD WAS AMERICA'S FIRST LADY FOR ONLY TWO SHORT YEARS, SHE CREATED A LEGACY THAT outdistances those of presidential wives with four times her length of service. Whether the subject was premarital sex, abortion, women's rights, her own breast cancer, or, finally, her recovery from an alarming dependence on drugs and alcohol, Ford spoke her mind—and her heart—with a nonpartisan candor that, coming on the heels of the Watergate scandal, was like a fresh breeze blowing into the stuffy backrooms of official Washington. ¶ Within days of taking up residence in the White House, the former model and Martha Graham dancer made headlines when she told an interviewer that she "wouldn't be surprised" if her 18-year-old daughter told her she was having an affair. An honest answer—but, in 1974, an impolitic one. Angry letters and telephone calls poured into the White House protesting her comments (which had also included an endorsement of legal abortion). ¶ Only weeks after the teen-sex blowup, Ford stunned the nation with another revelation: She had been diagnosed with breast cancer and would undergo an emergency mastectomy followed by chemotherapy. In going public with her illness, Ford single-handedly did more to raise awareness about breast cancer than decades' worth of public-service campaigns. Because of her, millions of women visited their doctors; countless more undertook regular self-examinations. ¶ In 1978, a year after her husband left office, another crisis and another brave personal admission set in motion what would become her greatest accomplishment. After being confronted by her worried family, Ford admitted that after nearly 15 years of dependence on prescription pills and a regular evening cocktail to alleviate chronic pain from arthritis and a pinched nerve in her neck, she had grown addicted. She checked herself into a California naval hospital specializing in substance abuse treatment.

Four years later, she founded the Betty Ford Center, an 80-bed residential drug-treatment facility in Rancho Mirage, California. Once again, Ford had taken a personal misfortune and, through her courage, given inspiration to millions. In the process, she did something even more significant: She changed the public perception of chemical addiction from a depravity to, simply, a disease.

betty Ford

helen Keller

1880—1968

HELEN KELLER REMAINS UNSURPASSED AS A SYMBOL OF TRIUMPH OVER PHYSICAL DISABILITY. INSEPARABLY ENTWINED WITH HER STORY IS THAT OF THE WOMAN WHO GAVE KELLER the tools to surmount her deafness and blindness (the result of a childhood bout with scarlet fever). Before Anne Sullivan—an orphan who had been born nearly blind herself—entered her life, when she was seven, Keller "had neither a will nor an intellect," as she later recalled. Sullivan broke through Keller's isolation by teaching her headstrong charge not only that the water that gushed onto her hand had a name, as did everything else she touched, but that her teacher could give them to her. ¶ Under Sullivan's guidance, Keller went on to study at New York's Horace Mann School and the Wright-Humason School for the Deaf, learning to speak by feeling the lip and tongue movements of her instructors and copying them to make similar sounds. She mastered Braille in Greek, Latin, French, and German as well as English. (Until Keller, the annals of medicine had recorded only one blind deaf-mute child who had learned to communicate verbally.) ¶ In 1900, Keller enrolled at Radcliffe, relying on Sullivan to spell out every lecture in her hands. Between classes she wrote *The Story of My Life*, published in 1903. When she graduated, *cum laude*, Sullivan stood on the podium beside her. ¶ Despite Sullivan's marriage to literary critic John Albert Macy (which ended in 1915), she continued to travel, teach, and lecture with Keller, who became an eloquent advocate for women's suffrage, the rights of the handicapped, and other liberal causes. "Life," Keller wrote in one of her many books, "is either a daring adventure, or nothing." Hers was most certainly the former, pursued with courage, commitment, and a total lack of self-pity.

> "
>
> **I thank God**
>
> **for my handicaps,**
>
> **for through them,**
>
> **I have found**
>
> **myself, my work,**
>
> **and my God.**
>
> "

m a r i a

Montessori

1870—1952 CONTEMPORARY PRIMARY EDUCATION DERIVES ITS FORM LARGELY FROM THE PIONEERING ITALIAN EDUCATOR MARIA MONTESSORI. IT WAS MONTESSORI WHO INTRODUCED TO CHILDREN'S CLASSROOMS SUCH NOW COMMONPLACE accouterments as child-size tables and chairs, lively colors, and developmental learning games. And it was she who first trained teachers to approach early education as a cooperative endeavor in which the kindergarten-age child should be guided but not lectured to or blamed. As her biographer Rita Kramer correctly observes, Montessori "belongs on any list of those whose existence shaped our century." And,

adds Kramer, "the fact that she was a woman, born in Italy 30 years before the end of the last century, makes that fact even more remarkable." ¶ Italy's first woman doctor, Montessori developed an interest in children with learning disabilities, becoming convinced of the value of manipulative materials and age-appropriate sensory stimulation in helping them learn. In 1907 she opened an experimental school in a Roman slum to test her principles on inner-city preschoolers without handicaps. They made remarkable progress in reading and writing. ¶ Explaining her system in the 1912 book *The Montessori Method*, Montessori denounced traditional schools where "children, like butterflies mounted on pins, are fastened each to his place." Essentially, the Montessori Method exploits a child's natural desire to learn with minimal intervention from a teacher. Enormously influential, the book launched an international educational reform movement. ¶ The Montessori movement has influenced early-childhood education to such a degree that there is probably not a day-care center or kindergarten classroom in America that does not incorporate at least some of Montessori's techniques and progressive ideas into its curriculum.

1948—

ON JANUARY 22, 1973, THE SUPREME COURT OF THE UNITED STATES HANDED DOWN ONE OF THE MOST SIGNIFICANT DECISIONS IN AMERICAN LEGAL HISTORY. RULING ON A PAIR of class action suits known collectively as *Roe v. Wade*, the justices decreed that abortion was a Constitutionally-protected right. ¶ Easily lost in the fiery debate surrounding the issue of abortion is the fact that the landmark case was a civil action involving very real women. "Jane Roe" was a Texan named Norma McCorvey. Unmarried, pregnant, and penniless, the 21-year-old (she used an alias to protect her privacy) decided in 1969 to challenge an 1854 Texas law that prohibited abortion except to save a woman's life. Her attorneys argued that the law violated a woman's Constitutional right to privacy, which they interpreted to include the right to decide whether or not to carry a pregnancy to term. ¶ *Doe v. Bolton*, the second case considered under the umbrella of *Roe v. Wade*, involved a young Atlanta woman who, poor and pregnant for the fourth time (she placed her first three children with adoption agencies), had been denied an abortion. (Although abortion was technically legal in Georgia, obtaining the procedure nevertheless required case-by-case approval by a panel of doctors, which was usually withheld.) Her lawyer argued that the state of Georgia's baroque abortion laws interfered with a woman's freedom to seek medical care and also with a physician's freedom to provide it—a violation, she contended, of the Fourteenth Amendment, which prohibits states from abridging the privileges of American citizens. ¶ The cases came before the Supreme Court in 1971. At the time, there were only 8,000 to 10,000 *legal* abortions being performed annually in the United States—out of what experts estimated to be between 1 and 1.5 million abortions in all.

❝

I'm pro-life. I think I have always been pro-life. I just didn't know it.

❞

In 31 states (including McCorvey's Texas), abortion in almost any form was strictly prohibited. More than a year passed before the Supreme Court released its historic ruling. (By then, both McCorvey and Doe had delivered their unwanted children and given them up for adoption.) ¶ McCorvey herself left a complicated legacy. In 1995, she abruptly changed her position, joining the staff of the anti-abortion group Operation Rescue and taking part in pro-life demonstrations (though she continued to endorse a woman's right to an abortion in the first trimester of pregnancy). Her actions underscored the fact that 25 years had done little to quiet the passions aroused by the landmark decision she set in motion.

j a n e Roe

margaret Sanger

1883—1966

EARLY IN THE CENTURY, UNWANTED PREGNANCIES WERE A FACT OF LIFE IN THE OVERCROWDED TENEMENTS OF NEW YORK CITY'S LOWER EAST SIDE. SO WERE CHILD ABUSE, NEGLECT, AND THE premature deaths of impoverished women from self-administered abortions. ¶ Exposed to these everyday tragedies in her work as a midwife and nurse, Margaret Sanger vowed to educate American women about birth control, a phrase she coined around 1914. When she embarked on this lifelong crusade, contraception was a forbidden subject. Doctors refused to talk about it. Organized churches rejected it. And, it was a criminal offense to share information about it through the mail. Sanger refused to let these strictures deter her. "If women are ever going to have a satisfactory sex life," Sanger said, "we have to get control over reproduction. Having a baby every time we sleep with our husbands is literally killing women before their time." ¶ Sanger founded her own radical journal, the *Woman Rebel,* in 1914. She wrote openly about contraception, and, predictably, the journal ran into legal trouble. Accused of violating the postal code, Sanger fled to England in 1914 rather than stand trial. Before leaving, however, Sanger published the first pamphlet ever, in English, to include detailed "how-to" information about contraception. ¶ Upon her return to the United States, Sanger suffered a terrible blow: the death by pneumonia of her 5-year-old daughter. Although this tragedy created public sympathy for her cause—and probably contributed to the New York District Attorney's decision to drop the earlier charges against her—Sanger's legal problems did not end. ¶ In 1916, she and her younger sister, Ethel Byrne, a nurse, opened America's first birth control clinic in Brooklyn. After nine days and some 500 clients (nearly all of them married mothers desperate to avoid further pregnancies), the clinic was shut down and Sanger and Byrne sent to jail to await the trial that would make "the birth control sisters" national figures. In a landmark ruling, the court decided that doctors could dispense contraceptive advice to women as an antidote to venereal disease. ¶ Sanger went on to found what would become the Planned Parenthood Federation of America and to publish *The Birth Control Review.* In 1952, she got a friend, the heiress Katherine McCormick, to subsidize the research for a female-controlled oral contraceptive. Sanger remained an outspoken advocate of women's reproductive rights until her death in 1966.

[*Margaret Sanger spread the word on birth control, often landing in legal hot water. At a 1929 Boston gathering (right) she taped her mouth shut to demonstrate how she felt about censorship.*]

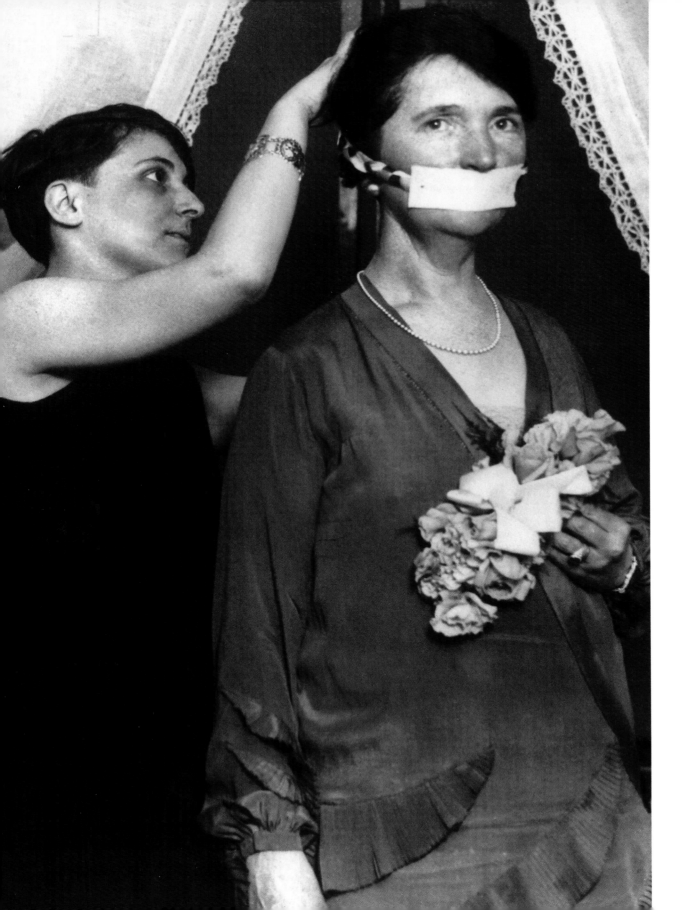

66

The most

important force in

the remaking of

the world is a free

motherhood.

99

> "
> This is Seagull.
>
> I see the horizon.
>
> A light blue,
>
> a blue band.
>
> This is the Earth.
>
> How beautiful it is!
> "

1937— FOR SHEER BRAVADO, LITTLE CAN MATCH THE GAME OF INTERSTELLAR ONE-UPMANSHIP PLAYED BETWEEN THE SOVIET UNION AND the United States in the late 1950s and early '60s. After the Soviets deployed Sputnik, the world's first man-made satellite, in 1957, the Americans responded by creating NASA. In 1961, the Soviets launched cosmonaut Yuri Gagarin into orbit. The Americans countered with astronaut Alan Shepard's suborbital flight a few weeks later, and John Glenn's orbit nine months after that. But NASA had no immediate answer for the Soviet's ace in the hole. She was Valentina Tereshkova, a 26-year-old, blond, blue-eyed textiles-worker-turned-cosmonaut. In 1963, Tereshkova, code-named the Seagull, became the first female pioneer of what has been called "the last frontier." ¶ "In space, too, our men will not feel lonely now," proclaimed Tereshkova, who triumphantly returned to terra firma after orbiting Earth 48 times during her three-day mission. "Let them feel there, too, friendly womanly support." ¶ "Womanly support" seriously understated the case. During time in orbit, Tereshkova braved the same rigors of weightless space travel as her macho comrades. Alone at the controls, she piloted her craft through extremes of heat and cold, following an orbit that took her as many as 145 miles above Earth. By the time she reentered the atmosphere, Tereshkova had smashed the space flight records of all of America's astronauts combined. The girl from a small village in western Russia clearly had the right stuff. ¶ Soviet Premier Nikita Khrushchev was thrilled to have beaten the Americans to another milestone, but Tereshkova's flight was more than a public relations coup. It was a victory for all women. With her success, another significant barrier fell.

valentina
Tereshkova

Timeline

What a difference a century makes! Women started out this century laced into corsets, without the vote, with a life expectancy of just over 50 years. Now we're orbiting the earth, truly becoming partners with men in positions of leadership, looking to a future of better opportunity and recognition for our daughters and granddaughters. It's been a perilous and wonderful journey.

1900s

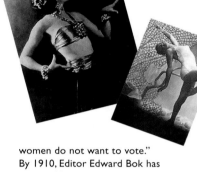

Ziegfeld Girls

Home Defenders' Army in a campaign to smash saloons across the country with a hatchet.

A *Ladies' Home Journal* article addressing the movement for college education for women answers no to the question, "Is a College Education The Best for Our Girls?" The magazine's stance will change within the next decade.

'01

Hubert Booth, a British bridge builder and designer, invents the first electric vacuum cleaner, which sucks dirt out of houses via a long tube to the street.

Beloved Queen Victoria, the longest reigning British monarch in history, dies at age 81.

Organized prenatal care in America begins in Boston.

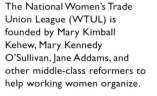

Queen Victoria

'02

Ida Tarbell begins publishing her *History of the Standard Oil Company* in installments in *McClure's*. Pioneering the journalistic style known as muckraking, she exposes Standard Oil's control of the industry with research that will contribute to the breakup of the company by order of the United States Supreme Court in 1911.

The International Woman's Conference in Washington, D.C., creates a committee for suffrage.

Beatrix Potter publishes *The Tale of Peter Rabbit*, which will become the best-selling children's book of all time.

'03

Maggie Lena Walker, of the St. Luke Penny Savings Bank in Richmond, Virginia, becomes the nation's first female bank president.

THE AMERICAN WOMAN, 1900
- TOTAL U.S. POPULATION: 76.1 MILLION
- TOTAL U.S. FEMALE POPULATION: 37.2 MILLION
- LIFE EXPECTANCY FOR WOMEN: 50.7 YEARS
- MEDIAN AGE AT WHICH A WOMAN MARRIES FOR THE FIRST TIME: 21.6
- COST OF A DOZEN EGGS: 20.7¢

The International Ladies' Garment Workers' Union is founded in New York City to protect workers in the women's garment industry, who typically earn 30 cents a day and work 70 hours a week.

Carry Nation, a prohibitionist from Kansas, begins leading the

Model-T Ford

The National Women's Trade Union League (WTUL) is founded by Mary Kimball Kehew, Mary Kennedy O'Sullivan, Jane Addams, and other middle-class reformers to help working women organize.

'04

Lillian D. Wald, Florence Kelley, and other reformers establish the National Child Labor Committee to work for anti-child-labor legislation.

Ethel Barrymore, the most critically acclaimed stage actress in America, appears on the cover of *Ladies' Home Journal* in a portrait painted by society painter John Singer Sargent. The magazine offers prints of the portrait ("rolled in a tube") to readers for 10 cents.

Russian immigrant and seamstress Lane Bryant is the first merchant to sell ready-to-wear maternity clothes. Her New York store will grow into a national chain that caters to large-size and pregnant women.

'05

U.S. geneticist Nettie Stevens identifies the X and Y chromosomes, pinpointing their role in determining the sex of an embryo.

Austrian pacifist Bertha von Suttner is the first woman to be awarded a Nobel Peace Prize.

In an article for *Ladies' Home Journal*, former president Grover Cleveland declares that "Sensible and responsible

women do not want to vote." By 1910, Editor Edward Bok has reversed his position on women's suffrage, publishing Jane Addams's landmark article, "Why Women Should Vote."

The hugely popular American actress Maude Adams opens in New York in the title role of *Peter Pan*, which playwright J.M. Barrie has written with her talents in mind.

The first commercial spermicidal jellies are marketed.

'06

In the social event of the year, Alice Roosevelt, the irrepressible 21-year-old daughter of President Theodore

The Jewel Electric Washer

First electric washing machine

Roosevelt and the most glamorous woman in the country, marries 39-year-old Congressman Nicholas Longworth.

Permanent waves are introduced in England; they take 8 to 12 hours and cost $1,000.

Ladies' Home Journal publishes a series of groundbreaking articles on venereal disease, causing 75,000 readers to cancel their subscriptions.

Beatrix Potter's *Peter Rabbit*

the fashion for thinness in women.

The first electric washing machine and the first home vacuum cleaner, manufactured by W. H. Hoover, are introduced.

'07

Washington, D.C., social worker Emily Bissell designs and prints the first Christmas seals, which she sells for a penny apiece. Within a year, the Christmas Seal drive has raised $120,000 for children with tuberculosis.

THE MAGAZINE WITH A MILLION
THE LADIES' HOME JOURNAL

JANUARY 1905
THE CURTIS PUBLISHING COMPANY, PHILADELPHIA

Ethel Barrymore adorns a 1905 *LHJ* cover

Mary Mallon, a.k.a. "Typhoid Mary," is captured after being linked to 25 cases of typhoid. Her case raises public awareness that a healthy person can be a carrier of a deadly contagious disease.

The Ziegfeld Follies debut on Broadway, showcasing tall, slender beauties in marked contrast to the plump, buxom burlesque girls of the past. The revue's popularity helps create

'08

Ladies' Home Journal editor Edward Bok conducts a crusade in the magazine for public health, decrying public drinking cups and unwrapped candy. "What do you eat with your candy," he asked, "typhoid germs or the bacilli of tuberculosis?" Unwrapped candy soon disappears from store shelves.

Henry Ford unveils the Model-T, a car designed to be affordable by the middle- and working-classes.

'09

Social reformers Mary White Ovington and Ida Wells-Barnett help found the National Association for the Advancement of Colored People (NAACP).

Selma Lagerlöf of Sweden, best known for her novel *Gösta Berlings Saga*, becomes the first woman to be awarded the Nobel Prize for literature.

German housewife Melitta Bentz invents the drip method of coffeemaking as a better-tasting alternative to perked coffee and begins marketing the Melitta drip coffeemaker.

1910s

THE AMERICAN WOMAN, 1910
• TOTAL U.S. POPULATION: 92.4 MILLION
• TOTAL U.S. FEMALE POPULATION: 44.8 MILLION
• LIFE EXPECTANCY FOR WOMEN: 53.2 YEARS
• MEDIAN AGE AT WHICH A WOMAN MARRIES FOR THE FIRST TIME: 21.6
• COST OF A DOZEN EGGS: 33.7¢

French designer Paul Poiret introduces slits into the narrow, ankle-length skirts of the day, creating "tango skirts" (so named for the dance that is becoming popular).

New York secretary Florence Nightingale Graham changes her name to Elizabeth Arden and opens a beauty salon on Fifth Avenue with a trademark red door. It is so successful that she eventually launches a cosmetics line that numbers more than 300 items.

'11

A fire at the Triangle Shirtwaist Company in New York City kills 146 workers, mostly women. Public outrage at the sweatshop conditions in the factory before

World War I call to work posters

the fire leads to much-needed labor reforms.

Charles Kettering invents an electric self-starter on automobiles that renders them safe for women to drive.

Harriet Quimby becomes America's first female licensed airplane pilot. In 1912, she becomes the first woman to fly

Triangle Shirtwaist fire

across the English Channel. She dies later in the year in an accident at a flying exhibition.

Woodbury, the first company to market facial soap as opposed to just ordinary soap, debuts its advertising slogan, "A Skin You Love to Touch."

'12

Women textile workers in Lawrence, Massachusetts, join with men (who work the same hours as they do, but are paid more) in a strike organized by Elizabeth Gurley Flynn of

World War I call to work posters

the Industrial Workers of the World. It provokes one of the bloodiest anti-union crackdowns in American history, but the workers prevail, winning raises of up to 25 percent. Soon after, Massachusetts passes the nation's first minimum-wage law.

The Girl Guides of America, renamed the Girl Scouts in 1923, is begun by Juliette Gordon Low, who started the Girl Guides in England in 1910.

"Slimming" becomes a pastime of American women, who begin to diet and exercise to conform to the ideal of what fashion writers call the "new beauty," in whom "thinness triumphs."

'13

Feminist Alice Paul organizes a suffrage parade in the nation's capital on the day preceding Woodrow Wilson's inauguration.

Ladies' Home Journal publishes one of the first articles ever to warn of the importance of

Suffragette

early detection in the treatment of cancer.

'14

Mother's Day is designated a national holiday, to occur on the second Sunday in May.

U.S. inventor Polly Jacobs obtains a patent for the first modern "backless" brassiere, consisting of a piece of cord, two handkerchiefs, and a strand of ribbon. Most women are still wearing whalebone or steel corsets.

The Women's Peace Parade is held in N.Y.C. to protest World War I.

'15

The International Congress of Women meets at the Hague to discuss approaches to ending World War I, and in America Carrie Chapman Catt and Jane Addams help create the Women's Peace Party.

Lipstick in metal tubes is packaged and sold for the first time.

Permanent waves administered in hair salons become popular, with such prominent women as First Lady Edith Bolting Wilson

paying as much as $120 for her curly new look.

'16

U.S. pacifist/feminist politician Jeanette Rankin is elected to Congress from Montana, becoming the first woman in the House of Representatives. The following year, she is the sole dissenting voice when the United States declares (a popular) war on Germany.

English birth control activist Marie Stopes publishes her controversial best-seller *Married Love*, in which she argues that wives have as much right to sexual satisfaction as their husbands. This idea will help launch a sexual revolution during the Roaring Twenties.

'17

As the U.S. enters World War I, American women go to work in iron and steel mills, chemical plants, foundries, lumber mills, munitions factories, and auto factories. None of them are admitted to unions, and all of them are paid less than their male coworkers.

American women are encouraged to donate their

World War I call to work posters

Skin-So-Soft ad

You too can have the charm of "A Skin you love to touch"

"FAREWELL TO AGE"

Elizabeth Arden —for skin like the petals of the lily

Elizabeth Arden ad

steel-reinforced corsets (which are being rendered obsolete by the modern bra) to the war effort. The donations yield 28,000 tons of steel—enough for two battleships.

The exotic dancer Mata Hari is executed by firing squad after being convicted of spying for the Germans. Her treachery is responsible for an estimated 50,000 Allied casualties.

Amanda "Ma" Ferguson becomes governor of Texas when she fills the vacancy left by her impeached husband. She is the first woman governor in American history; she will be elected in her own right in 1924.

A U.S. Department of Labor study finds that childbirth is the second leading cause of death for women ages 15 to 44. Tuberculosis is the first.

'18

President Wilson declares support of the national women's suffrage amendment, which he says is urgently needed as a "war measure."

'19

A woman's suffrage amendment passes in Congress and goes to the states for ratification.

1920s

The liberated woman

THE AMERICAN WOMAN, 1920
- TOTAL U.S. POPULATION: 106.5 MILLION
- TOTAL U.S. FEMALE POPULATION: 52.2 MILLION
- LIFE EXPECTANCY FOR WOMEN: 57.4 YEARS
- MEDIAN AGE AT WHICH A WOMAN MARRIES FOR THE FIRST TIME: 21.2
- RATIO OF MARRIAGES TO DIVORCES: 10.3:1.5
- PERCENTAGE OF WOMEN IN THE WORKFORCE: 23.1 %
- COST OF A DOZEN EGGS: 68.1¢
- AVERAGE COST OF A HOUSE: $4,113

Spurred by euphoria over the passage of the 19th Amendment, some 283,000 women are enrolled in college, representing nearly 47 percent of all undergraduates. However, their course work is usually stereotyped according to

First domestic steam iron

gender, and their numbers will steadily decline over the next four decades.

The 19th Amendment, giving American women the right to vote, is signed into law.

The National League of Women Voters is established.

Joan of Arc is canonized.

The modest use of makeup is now common among "respectable" American women.

'21

The first Miss America Pageant is held. The winner (chosen from just seven contestants) is 16-year-old Margaret Gorman of Washington, D.C. She stands 5'1" tall and weighs 108 pounds.

First in-home refrigeration

The Sheppard-Towner Maternity and Infancy Protection Act, designed to educate women about

pregnancy and child care, passes Congress after heavy lobbying by women's reform groups and heavy opposition from the medical establishment.

Betty Crocker is introduced to promote Gold Medal Flour. A male correspondent for the company answers mail addressed to the name until 1936. Over time, the portrait of the ever popular Betty Crocker is repainted six times to reflect changing fashion.

Kimberly-Clark Company begins marketing Kotex, the first commercially available sanitary napkin.

Wyeth introduces SMA, the first commercially available prepared baby formula. As competing brands come on the market, breast-feeding among American women rapidly declines.

'22

The "flapper" emerges and becomes the quintessential image of the 1920s female: She bobs her hair, binds her breasts, swears, smokes cigarettes, and wears knee-length dresses, rouge, and lipstick.

Rebecca Felton becomes the first woman to occupy a seat in the U.S. Senate following her husband's death.

The Bat Mitzvah, a feminine counterpart to the Bar Mitzvah ceremony for 13-year-old Jewish boys, makes its debut in America.

'23

Feminist Alice Paul introduces her version of the Equal Rights Amendment at a meeting of the National Woman's Party in Seneca Falls, New York. The amendment is introduced to Congress later in the year.

The powerfully energetic Charleston becomes popular across America.

Frigidaire introduces a home refrigerator, making safer food storage widely available.

The diaphragm contraceptive is introduced in the United States.

'24

The Supreme Court upholds protective legislation forbidding late-night work by women.

Above: Beauty pageants become popular
Right: First Miss America

'25

The right of a married woman to keep her birth names is recognized by the U.S. State Department.

Smoking is fashionable for women, requiring such chic accessories as long, jeweled cigarette holders.

The National Academy of Sciences accepts its first woman member, Dr. Florence Sabin, a physician who fought to modernize public health laws.

African-American dancer Josephine Baker becomes the

toast of Paris in her erotic song-and-dance show, *La Revue Nègre*.

'26

The first domestic steam irons are available to U.S. households at a price of $10; the pop-up electric toaster is introduced.

'27

Gerber Baby Foods is founded in Michigan. It is the first company to market reasonably priced commercial baby foods sold in grocery stores rather than pharmacies.

Women voters

The "Pap" test for early detection of cervical and uterine cancer is developed by George Papanicolau.

The Ascheim-Zonadek urine pregnancy test (the "rabbit test") is developed.

'28

Track and field for women is introduced at the Amsterdam Summer Olympic Games.

'29

With the stock-market crash, women's hemlines plunge back to midcalf.

Home hair color is introduced (Nestlé Colorinse in ten shades) in Europe.

Luxite Hosiery

Hosiery ad

1930s

Convenience foods introduced

THE AMERICAN WOMAN, 1930
- TOTAL U.S. POPULATION: 123.1 MILLION
- TOTAL U.S. FEMALE POPULATION: 60.8 MILLION
- LIFE EXPECTANCY FOR WOMEN: 60.9
- MEDIAN AGE AT WHICH A WOMAN MARRIES FOR THE FIRST TIME: 21.3
- RATIO OF MARRIAGES TO DIVORCES: 10.4:1.7
- AVERAGE HOUSEHOLD SIZE: 3.9 PEOPLE
- PERCENTAGE OF WOMEN IN THE WORKFORCE: 23.1 PERCENT
- COST OF A DOZEN EGGS: 44.5¢
- AVERAGE COST OF A HOUSE: $3,900

Trousers become acceptable attire for women who play golf and ride horses.

United Airlines introduces flight attendants to serve food and beverages and to comfort passengers. None can be taller than 5'4" or weigh more than 115 pounds.

Frozen foods (Birdseye Frosted Foods) go on sale for the first time, but they are too expensive (a package of peas costs 35¢) for most American families while few grocers have freezers for holding them. Pre-sliced bread, labeled Wonder Bread, is also introduced.

A National Education Association survey of U.S. school districts reveals that 77 percent won't hire married women as teachers; 63 percent will fire the woman if she gets married.

Women's ovulation patterns are revealed by Japanese scientists, and the tiny human egg cell is viewed under a microscope for the first time.

In a papal encyclical Pope Pius XI condemns the use of artificial birth control by Roman Catholics.

Italian-born Parisian couturier Elsa Schiaparelli introduces the use of "zippers" (the patent will expire in 1931) in her clothing line.

'31

The U.S. birth rate falls as a result of the Depression.

Nevada institutes "quickie" divorces. In 1943 the Supreme Court rules them valid in all states.

American women increasingly assume their husbands' names upon marriage. By decade's end, name changes will be nearly automatic, something that woman just naturally do.

Verne "Jackie" Mitchell becomes the first woman to play major league baseball for the Memphis Lookouts of the Southern Association. In an exhibition game, she strikes out both Babe Ruth and Lou Gehrig.

First dishwasher

'32

One Man's Family, the first "soap opera," so called for its soap-manufacturer sponsors, debuts on NBC radio.

'33

Windex window cleaner is introduced.

Massachusetts innkeeper Ruth Wakefield invents Toll House cookies.

'34

Ohio Supreme Court judge Florence Ellinwood Allen

Wearing pants becomes acceptable

becomes the first woman federal judge when President Roosevelt appoints her to the U.S. Sixth Circuit Court of Appeals.

Six-year-old Shirley Temple becomes Hollywood's top box-office star.

Nylon, the first completely synthetic fiber, is invented.

The female hormone progesterone is isolated.

'35

Gretchen B. Schoeleber becomes the first woman member of the New York Stock exchange.

Bra cup sizes (A–D) are introduced by Leona Lax, a designer for Warner Brothers, a Bridgeport, Connecticut, company.

'36

Tampax, the first commercially available tampon, is introduced.

Shirley Temple

Birth control information is ruled to be no longer obscene under the U.S. Comstock Act.

The U.S. Supreme Court strikes down as unconstitutional a 1933 minimum wage law for women, but the following year upholds the principle of such a wage.

'37

The American Medical Association recognizes birth control as legitimate subject matter for medical schools, and the first state contraceptive clinic opens in North Carolina.

The invention of the steel shopping cart launches a revolution in food shopping.

'38

The U.S. Fair Labor Standards Act guarantees a minimum wage for women, but many in domestic service and agricultural labor are unaffected.

'39

The U.S. Department of Agriculture establishes the first food stamp program.

A new U.S. Food, Drug and Cosmetic Act requires drug manufacturers to test products for safety before marketing.

The first synthetic estrogen is created.

The California Perfume Company renames itself Avon Products after Shakespeare's birthplace, Stratford-on-Avon. The cosmetic company's door-to-door salespeople—who will eventually number 1.5 million, making Avon the country's largest employer of women—will become known as "Avon Ladies."

The first fully automated electric washing machine, the first pressure cooker, and the first automatic dishwasher are introduced.

1940s

First bikini from Paris

THE AMERICAN WOMAN, 1940
- TOTAL U.S. POPULATION: 132.1 MILLION
- TOTAL U.S. FEMALE POPULATION: 65.8 MILLION
- LIFE EXPECTANCY FOR WOMEN: 65.9 YEARS
- MEDIAN AGE AT WHICH A WOMAN MARRIES FOR THE FIRST TIME: 21.5
- RATIO OF MARRIAGES TO DIVORCES:12.1:3.5
- AVERAGE NUMBER OF CHILDREN BORN TO AN AMERICAN WOMAN: 2.3
- PERCENTAGE OF WOMEN IN THE WORKFORCE: 35.8 %
- COST OF A DOZEN EGGS: 33.1¢
- AVERAGE COST OF A HOUSE: $4,900

Women in the workforce posters

Ida May Fuller, a 35-year-old Vermont widow, becomes the first recipient of Social Security.

Limited numbers of nylon stockings go on sale nationwide, generating stampedes and near-hysteria. Wash and wear clothing becomes available.

'41

As the United States enters World War II, some 4,000 women are working in the aircraft industry. Pop song "Rosie the Riveter" symbolizes these pioneering women.

Ladies' Home Journal launches its famous slogan, "Never Underestimate The Power Of A Woman."

'42

The U.S. Congress creates the Women's Army Corps (WAAC, changed to WAC in 1943) and Women Accepted for Voluntary Emergency Service (WAVES).

In the United States, women grow victory gardens and hold scrap metal drives to help the war effort.

The U.S. National War Labor Board issues General Order 16, urging voluntary equalization of female and male wages.

U.S. doctor Elizabeth McCoy discovers a way to increase production of penicillin; Dr. Dorothy Fennel helps develop a more powerful strain of the drug called penicillin fenneliae.

Betty Grable

U.S. obstetrics introduces the use of spinal anesthesia, permitting women to undergo childbirth fully conscious while feeling nothing from the waist down.

Hordes of teenage bobby-soxers swoon outside New York's Paramount Theater, where singer Frank Sinatra appears in an eight-week engagement.

Actress Betty Grable becomes the favorite pinup girl of American servicemen.

'43

The Women Air Force Service Pilots (WASPS) is founded.

Wonder Woman comic books debut with a character designed to be a "female superman."

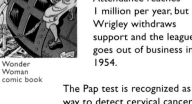
Wonder Woman comic book

Chicago Cubs owner Philip K. Wrigley founds the All-American Girls' Baseball League. Attendance reaches 1 million per year, but Wrigley withdraws support and the league goes out of business in 1954.

The Pap test is recognized as way to detect cervical cancer by medical establishment, but few doctors use it on healthy, nonpregnant women. (In 1947, *Ladies' Home Journal* helps launch a media campaign urging women to demand the simple test that saves lives.)

Doctors begin to prescribe diethyl-stilbestrol (DES), a hormone intended to prevent miscarriage in pregnant women. Later it is shown to cause a wide variety of medical problems in both sons and daughters born to those mothers.

'44

The wartime influx of females into the workforce peaks with 19 million women—nearly half of all American women—holding jobs outside the home. However, women in manufacturing jobs make 65 percent as much as their male coworkers.

A record 3.5 million women belong to labor unions—a marked increase from the 800,000 before the war.

English obstetrician Grantly Read publishes *Childbirth Without Fear: The Principles and Practices of Natural Childbirth*, helping to popularize the idea of childbirth without anesthesia.

'45

Women lose jobs as returning male soldiers reclaim their previous positions. The level of female employment will never return to its prewar level.

Secretary of Labor Lewis Schwellenbach urges legislation to ban wage differentials because of sex and claims that discrimination "depresses the whole wage structure."

"Rosie the Riveter"

Tupperware plastic products are introduced and sold exclusively at Tupperware Parties.

'46

The bikini bathing suit debuts at a fashion show in Paris. Named after the Bikini atoll, where hydrogen bomb testing has taken place, the suit is said to produce a similarly explosive effect on the male viewer.

The baby boom begins. By the time it ends in 1964, 76 million babies will have been born in the United States.

Dr. Benjamin Spock publishes *The Common Sense Book of Baby and Child Care*, which goes on to become a child-care bible for American mothers and the best-selling baby book in history. In 1954, Dr. Spock becomes a regular contributor to *Ladies' Home Journal*.

Tide, the first detergent strong enough for washing both clothes and dishes, is introduced by Procter & Gamble.

'47

Construction on the suburban New York housing development known as Levittown begins. The first houses there sell for $6,990.

Jane Russell in *The Outlaw*

The Army–Navy Nurse Act authorizes permanent commissions for U.S. military nurses.

Dior's "New Look," debuting in Paris, reintroduces lower hemlines and opulent use of fabric in women's fashions.

Hollywood star Jane Russell appears in *The Outlaw* wearing a special, cantilevered bra devised by aeronautical designer Howard Hughes to

The new hemline

Dior's "New Look"

maximize her bust and to minimize its bouncing.

Aluminum foil is invented; Ajax, a cleanser with silica sand, is introduced and quickly surpasses other household cleansers; Reddi-Whip, the first major aerosol food product, is introduced.

Dorothy Fuldheim of Cleveland, Ohio, becomes the first female television news anchor.

'48

The United Nations General Assembly passes the Universal Declaration of Human Rights, drafted by Eleanor Roosevelt.

'49

Harvard Law School authorizes the admission of women.

General Mills and Pillsbury introduce prepared cake mixes; Pillsbury launches its annual Bake-Off, a contest to help develop recipes using flour.

Iva Toguri d'Aquino, one of 13 American women known as "Tokyo Rose" for reading Japanese propaganda over the radio to American GIs, is acquitted on eight counts of treason, but found guilty of trying to undermine military morale and sentenced to 6 years in prison.

1950s

TV dinners make their debut

Hurricanes begin to be named after women.

Journalist and playwright Clare Boothe Luce is sworn in as ambassador to Italy, the most important diplomatic position ever to be awarded to a U.S. woman.

Ladies' Home Journal debuts the "first of a revealing new series on real-life marriages" entitled "Can This Marriage Be Saved?" It will become the longest continuously running column in magazine history.

Alfred Kinsey publishes *Sexual Behavior and the Human Female*, a follow-up to his landmark 1948 *Sexual Behavior in the Human Male.* An article in *Ladies' Home Journal* interprets the study's findings for American women.

Ultrasound, or high-frequency sound waves, is used successfully for the first time to study an unborn baby. It will come into wide diagnostic use beginning in 1978.

Shirley Polykoff of Foote, Cone & Belding advertising agency creates the classic "Does she...or doesn't she? Hair Color so natural only her hairdresser

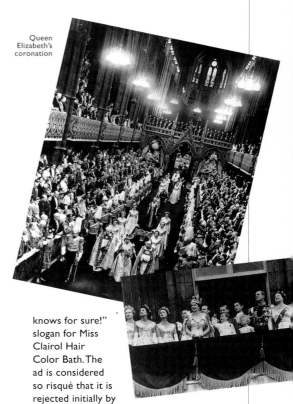
Queen Elizabeth's coronation

THE AMERICAN WOMAN, 1950
- TOTAL U.S. POPULATION: 151.7 MILLION
- TOTAL U.S. FEMALE POPULATION: 76.1 MILLION
- LIFE EXPECTANCY FOR WOMEN: 70.9 YEARS
- MEDIAN AGE AT WHICH A WOMAN MARRIES FOR THE FIRST TIME: 20.3
- RATIO OF MARRIAGES TO DIVORCES: 9.1 : 2.3
- AVERAGE NUMBER OF CHILDREN BORN TO AN AMERICAN WOMAN: 3.09
- PERCENTAGE OF WOMEN IN THE WORKFORCE: 35.7 %
- COST OF A DOZEN EGGS: 60.4¢
- AVERAGE COST OF A HOUSE: $9,650

continue to use her maiden name after marriage.

Maxwell House introduces the first modern instant coffee; Minute Rice is introduced.

'51

U.S. housewife Marion Donovan invents the Boater, the first disposable diaper.

French obstetricians Fernand Lamaze and Pierre Vellay introduce their method of "painless" childbirth, which will come to be known as the Lamaze method.

'52

U.S. medical researcher Dr. Dorothy Horstmann isolates the polio virus in its early stages, making it easier to develop a vaccine for the crippling disease, which has become a nationwide epidemic affecting more than 50,000 Americans.

Christine Jorgensen (born George Jorgensen) becomes the first transsexual to go public with details of her sex-change surgery in Denmark.

Stiletto heels are introduced by Italian designer Ferragamo. The shoes have a steel spike in the heel that makes possible their ultra-thin height.

'53

Queen Elizabeth II is coronated in Westminster Abbey.

Breast feeding is promoted

'54

The Miss America Pageant becomes the first nationally televised beauty contest.

Swanson markets the first frozen TV dinner (turkey). More than 10 million sell the first year.

'55

The Salk vaccine against polio is licensed for use. Millions of American children receive injections. Within five years, an even more effective oral vaccine will become available.

knows for sure!" slogan for Miss Clairol Hair Color Bath. The ad is considered so risqué that it is rejected initially by the all-male management of *Life* magazine and accepted only after it is endorsed by the magazine's female staff members.

'56

President Eisenhower calls for "equal pay for equal work without discrimination because of sex."

La Leche League International is formed to promote breast feeding, which has fallen out of favor and is now practiced by only 22 percent of American mothers.

The U.S. Census Bureau recognizes a woman's right to

The first Minute Rice

Sack Dress

Actress Grace Kelly marries Prince Rainier III of Monaco.

Josephine Holt Bay becomes the first woman to head a New York Stock Exchange member company, A.M. Kidder & Co.

'57

E.I. DuPont introduces Spandex, marketed by the name Lycra, for use in bras and the popular "panty girdle."

Despite physical threats, Arkansas State Press publisher Daisy Lee Bates continues her support of the "Little Rock Nine" in their crusade to desegregate the city's Central High School, which finally happens in 1959.

Stiletto heels

The "sack" dress and the new, three-quarter-length "car coat" become the vogue.

'58

Sweet 'n Low is the first commercial powdered sugar substitute.

'59

Hawaii, in becoming a state, is the first to pass a law requiring that married women take their husbands' last names.

Pantyhose are invented and marketed under the name Panti-Legs by Glen Raven Mills of Altamahaw, North Carolina.

Instant coffee

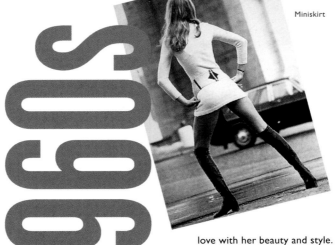

Miniskirt

1960s

THE AMERICAN WOMAN, 1960
- TOTAL U.S. POPULATION: 180.7 MILLION
- TOTAL U.S. FEMALE POPULATION: 91.4 MILLION
- LIFE EXPECTANCY FOR WOMEN: 73.2 YEARS
- MEDIAN AGE AT WHICH A WOMAN MARRIES FOR THE FIRST TIME: 20.3
- RATIO OF MARRIAGES TO DIVORCES: 9.2 : 2.5
- AVERAGE NUMBER OF CHILDREN BORN TO AN AMERICAN WOMAN: 3.65
- PERCENTAGE OF WOMEN IN THE WORKFORCE: 39.3 PERCENT
- COST OF A DOZEN EGGS: 57.3¢
- AVERAGE COST OF A HOUSE: $14,450

The first commercial birth control pill, Enovid, is approved by the Food and Drug Administration (FDA). Its development was funded after the early 1950s by U.S. philanthropist and feminist Katharine Dexter McCormick.

Teflon-coated cookware comes on the market and is an instant success.

'61

Jacqueline Bouvier Kennedy becomes first lady of the United States, and the public falls in love with her beauty and style. Among the fashions she helps popularize are the pillbox hat and the bouffant hairstyle.

President Kennedy creates the President's Commission on the Status of Women and names Eleanor Roosevelt chairwoman. When the President receives the report in 1963, he concedes that American women are discriminated against on account of their gender.

'62

The tranquilizer Thalidomide is removed from the market after it causes 12,000 malformations in infants born to mothers who took the drug while pregnant.

"The Pill"

The first silicone gel breast implants become available. By 1973, some 50,000 women will have had the gel bags implanted.

Ladies' Home Journal runs "New Weapons Against Breast Cancer," the first article in a major women's magazine to cover breast cancer.

'63

Congress passes the Equal Pay Act, requiring equal wages for men and women doing equal work.

Pope John XXIII, breaking tradition, allows five female delegates to attend the Vatican II conference, which will liberalize Roman Catholicism.

Texas entrepreneur Mary Kay Wagner founds her door-to-door cosmetics company, Mary Kay Cosmetics, Inc.

'64

The U.S. Civil Rights Act is passed.

Cigarettes, used by 40 percent of American adults, lose their glamour as the U.S. Surgeon General's Office issues its landmark report on the hazards of smoking.

'65

The "miniskirt" launches a hemline revolution. Other top fashions include bellbottom pants, white "go-go" boots,

Coretta Scott King at a memorial march

exposed knees, and textured stockings.

Lyndon Johnson's "Great Society" expands social welfare programs, creating Medicare, Medicaid, food stamps, and Project Head Start, a preschool education program for underprivileged children.

Twiggy

First Lady "Lady Bird" Johnson launches a movement to beautify America, beginning with a campaign to remove U.S. highway billboards on interstates and other highways not zoned for commercial or industrial use.

'66

Groups form to advance the cause of women's rights—most notably the National Organization for Women (NOW).

Pierced ears become fashionable for American women, as does Britain's "mod" look.

'67

Some 2,500 women protesting the Vietnam War storm the Pentagon in a rally organized by Women's Strike for Peace.

Senator Eugene McCarthy introduces the Equal Rights

Amendment in the U.S. Senate.

A group of women picket the Atlantic City site of the Miss America Pageant, arguing that the contest is offensive to women.

Seventeen-year-old Twiggy (née Leslie Hornby) shakes up the fashion scene with her beanpole figure and quirky looks.

President Johnson issues an executive order prohibiting sex discrimination in employment by the federal government and by contractors doing business with the federal government.

'68

U.S. civil rights activist Coretta Scott King leads a memorial march in Memphis for her slain husband Martin Luther King, Jr.

U.S. Equal Opportunity Commission rules that gender is not a requirement to be a flight attendant, allowing male flight attendants to be hired.

Ladies' Home Journal is the first mass-market women's magazine to feature a black woman, model Naomi Sims, on its cover.

'69

The Equal Employment Opportunity Commission revisions make it illegal to advertise many jobs under "male" and "female" headings.

The Doctor's Case Against the Pill, by Barbara Seaman, warns against the dangers of the birth-control pill. The book is credited with getting dosages of hormones in the pills lowered and in launching the women's health movement.

Lady Bird Johnson

1970s

THE AMERICAN WOMAN, 1970
- U.S. POPULATION: 204.9 MILLION
- TOTAL U.S. FEMALE POPULATION: 104.6 MILLION
- LIFE EXPECTANCY FOR WOMEN: 74.64 YEARS
- MEDIAN AGE AT WHICH A WOMAN MARRIES FOR THE FIRST TIME: 20.8
- RATIO OF MARRIAGES TO DIVORCES: 10.0 : 4.8
- AVERAGE NUMBER OF CHILDREN BORN TO AN AMERICAN WOMAN: 2.48
- PERCENTAGE OF WOMEN IN THE WORKFORCE: 46.3 PERCENT
- COST OF A DOZEN EGGS: 61.4¢
- AVERAGE COST OF A HOUSE: $32,100

In response to an 11-hour sit-in at the *Ladies' Home Journal* offices by 200 women protesting the content of women's magazines and demanding the resignation of editor John Mack Carter and the appointment of a female editor-in-chief, the magazine runs an eight-page insert titled "The New Feminism: A Special Section Prepared for the *Ladies' Home Journal* by the Women's Liberation Movement."

The Boston Women's Health Book Collective publishes *Our Bodies, Ourselves*, helping to raise

Diane Keaton and the "Annie Hall" look

consciousness about women's health issues. The book goes on to sell more than 3 million copies and be translated into 14 languages.

Two feminist classics, Germaine Greer's *The Female Eunuch* and Kate Millett's *Sexual Politics*, are published.

The calf-length "midi" skirt, touted as the hemline for spring, fails to catch on. This marks the beginning of the end of American women's automatic obedience to the hemline dictates of the fashion industry.

The *Mary Tyler Moore Show*, featuring Moore as Mary Richards, a happily single career woman, debuts on CBS on Saturday nights. It will run for seven successful seasons.

America's first no-fault divorce law is enacted in California.

'71

The Civil Service Commission rules that sex specification in federal jobs must be eliminated.

The Supreme Court rules that companies may not deny employment to women with small children unless they also do so to men.

The Supreme Court lets stand a U.S. circuit court ruling that

Mary Tyler Moore

company pension plans may not require women to retire before men.

'72

Title IX of the Higher Education Act, which calls for equal opportunities for both male and female students, is passed. It bans sex discrimination in educational programs receiving federal funds.

The U.S. Congress approves the Equal Rights Amendment, which would empower the government to ensure that rights are not abridged on the grounds of sex, and sends it to the states for ratification.

'73

The Supreme Court rules in Roe v. Wade that a woman's right to privacy

"is broad enough to encompass a woman's decision whether or not to terminate her pregnancy." The ruling strikes down all laws that prevent abortions in the first trimester.

The Federal Home Loan Bank Board ends discrimination against women when granting mortgage loans.

'74

The Dalkon shield intrauterine contraceptive device is withdrawn from the market as unsafe. Its maker, A.H. Robins, eventually declares bankruptcy in order to protect itself from numerous lawsuits.

California makes it legal for women to begin using the title Ms. rather than Mrs. or Miss.

The League of Women Voters decides to allow full membership to men.

Girls are admitted to Little League baseball teams for the first time.

Eleven women are ordained as Episcopal priests, though official sanction from the Church's ruling body comes only in 1976.

Roe v. Wade demonstrators pro and con

'75

The United Nations proclaims Woman's Year. In Berlin, the World Congress for International Woman's Year opens with almost 2,000 delegates from 141 countries.

ERA demonstration

Congress passes a bill to allow women admittance to the nation's military academies. The U.S. Coast Guard Academy becomes the first service academy to admit women.

'76

Women win 13 of 32 Rhodes Scholarships awarded to Americans in the first year they are open to women.

Congress passes the Hyde Amendment, limiting federal funding of abortions to those that save the life of the mother.

Cuisinart introduces the food processor.

'77

The "Annie Hall look" (oversized men's jackets and shirts, long skirts, baggy khakis, and loose neckties), derived from the Woody Allen

movie, becomes the epitome of funky chic.

Mammograms become widely available as a method of early detection of breast cancer.

Shere Hite publishes *The Hite Report* on women's sexuality, which becomes a best-seller.

'78

Englishwoman Lesley Brown gives birth to Louise Brown, the world's first "test-tube" baby.

Female sportswriters in the U.S. get permission to enter major league baseball locker rooms.

The National Coalition Against Violence is founded to help battered women.

In the largest such gathering in history, women demonstrators rally on the Mall in Washington, D.C., to support an extension of the 1979 deadline to ratify the Equal Rights Amendment, which is three states short of

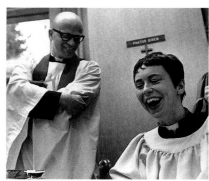

Woman priest

ratification. In response, Congress extends the deadline by 39 months.

'79

The U.S. National Weather Service begins naming half of all tropical storms and hurricanes after men rather than just women.

For the first time, more females than males are entering college.

Girls play in Little League baseball

1980s

The Vietnam War Memorial

The first Conference of the National Coalition Against Domestic Violence is held to protest spousal abuse.

The Defense Department extends full military veteran status to 16,000 women who served in the Women's Auxiliary Army Corps during World War II.

The FDA mandates labeling of tampon packages with warnings against toxic shock syndrome. Procter & Gamble withdraws its super-absorbent tampon, Rely, from the market, because it has been suspected of fostering the bacterium responsible for toxic shock syndrome, which has killed 25 people.

The National Institutes of Health issue a 500-page report analyzing the alarming rise in cesarean deliveries of babies, which are nearly twice as expensive and involve longer recovery times than vaginal deliveries. By 1988, more than one in four American babies will be born by cesarean section.

Dressing for success

'81

U.S. Congress withdraws Medicaid funding for abortions to end pregnancies caused by incest or rape; the Supreme Court upholds a law requiring doctors to notify a minor's parents before performing an abortion.

The Supreme Court rules that women can sue their employers for wage discrimination even if their jobs vary from those of their male coworkers.

The Equal Employment Opportunity Commission reports that women's earnings lag 60 percent behind those of men.

The National Collegiate Athletic Association (NCAA) sponsors its first women's championships.

'82

The Equal Rights Amendment is defeated, falling three states short of the necessary 38 for ratification by June 30.

A new Surgeon General's report calls cigarette smoking the chief preventable cause of death; for the second year in a row, more women than men smoke.

Liposuction, a surgical method of suctioning away fat, makes its debut in the United States.

The Vietnam War Memorial, designed by Maya Lin, a 21-year-old Yale architecture student, is dedicated in Washington, D.C. It quickly becomes the capital's most visited monument.

'83

A study by the American Society of Podiatrists reports that one in ten American women now wears a size 10 shoe or larger—a result of better nutrition, but also increased physical fitness.

Astronaut Sally Ride is the first American woman in space, spending six days as a crew member aboard the Challenger.

First Lady Nancy Reagan unveils her "Just Say No" slogan to fight drug use among teenagers as crack becomes a nationwide epidemic.

Condoms enjoy a revived popularity as protection against sexually transmitted diseases.

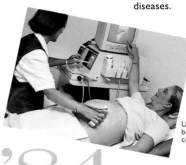

Ultrasound becomes commonplace

'84

New York Congresswoman Geraldine A. Ferraro joins Walter Mondale on the Democratic presidential ticket, becoming the first woman from a major party to run for vice president.

AIDS virus (HIV) is discovered. Geneticist Flossie Wong-Staal is the first to clone HIV.

Cosmonaut Svetlana Savitskaya is the first woman to walk in space; U.S. biologist Kathryn Sullivan is the second, and the first American woman to do so.

The use by pregnant women of ultrasound diagnostic procedures and amniocentesis, a procedure to identify chromosomal and genetic abnormalities in a fetus, becomes widespread.

'85

The FDA requires the makers of silicone gel breast implants to issue broader warnings on the dangers of their product.

Tipper Gore, the wife of Tennessee Senator Albert Gore, urges Congress to mandate labels for record albums containing "offensive lyrics."

A University of Pittsburgh study on breast cancer finds that lumpectomies plus radiation are as effective in preventing recurrence as mastectomies.

'86

The U.S. space shuttle Challenger, whose crew includes NASA scientist Judith Resnik and New Hampshire schoolteacher Christa McAuliffe (who was to become the first civilian in space), explodes 73 seconds after liftoff from Cape Canaveral in Florida.

The Supreme Court upholds Affirmative Action on the basis of race and gender.

In Meritor Savings Bank v. Vinson, the Supreme Court defines sexual harassment as a type of discrimination illegal under federal law.

'87

Supreme Court upholds the constitutionality of voluntary affirmative action programs for women in employment fields where they had previously been excluded.

The Supreme Court rules that Rotary Clubs must admit women.

The "Baby M" case, in which a biological mother who agreed to be artificially inseminated and to give birth to a child for another couple changed her mind about giving up her baby, highlights the murky legal issues surrounding surrogate motherhood (a practice covered by no existing laws). The New Jersey Supreme Court eventually gives

Astronaut Sally Ride

custody of the child to the biological father, grants the biological mother generous parental rights, and declares surrogacy contracts illegal.

Women own 30 percent of all U.S. businesses.

'88

Congress authorizes a memorial for female Vietnam veterans.

American Barbara Harris becomes the first female Episcopal bishop.

The FDA approves the cervical cap contraceptive; the drug RU486, which brings on miscarriage in the early months of pregnancy, is approved for use in France and China.

Florence Griffith-Joyner wins three gold medals and one silver medal at the Summer Olympics, setting sprint records that surpass those of any woman and come close to matching many men's records.

'89

In Webster v. Reproductive Health Services, the Supreme Court upholds states' rights to limit access to abortion—a victory for pro-life organizations and a major defeat for pro-choice groups.

The first Women's Olympic hockey team

1990s

THE AMERICAN WOMAN, 1990
- U.S. POPULATION: 249.4 MILLION
- TOTAL U.S. FEMALE POPULATION: 127.6 MILLION
- LIFE EXPECTANCY FOR WOMEN: 79.1 YEARS
- MEDIAN AGE AT WHICH A WOMAN MARRIES FOR THE FIRST TIME: 23.9
- RATIO OF MARRIAGES TO DIVORCES: 9.1 : 4.6
- AVERAGE NUMBER OF CHILDREN BORN TO AN AMERICAN WOMAN: 2.08
- PERCENTAGE OF WOMEN IN THE WORKFORCE: 58.9 PERCENT
- COST OF A DOZEN EGGS: $1.01
- AVERAGE COST OF A HOUSE: $86,529

Russian issue of LHJ

Dr. Antonia Novello becomes the first female Surgeon General in the United States.

To celebrate glasnost, Ladies' Home Journal publishes an issue in both Russian and English.

The FDA approves Norplant, the first major new form of contraception in over 20 years. The device, implanted under the skin of a woman's arm, releases

hormonal contraceptives slowly over a long period of time.

'91

Dr. Bernadine Healy becomes the first female director of the National Institutes of Health; the National Breast Cancer Coalition, dedicated to research on breast cancer, is founded. Within a year, the Coalition wins $300 million in additional funding, and has brought pressure on Congress to transfer $210 million in defense spending to research for breast cancer.

A Pentagon report reveals that at a convention in Las Vegas of the Tailhook Association of top U.S. Navy aviators, 83 women and at least seven men were sexually abused, and that such abuse was institutionally condoned.

'92

The House of Representatives approves a defense budget that includes a provision to allow women in the Air Force, Navy, and Marine Corps to fly combat aircraft for the first time.

Bill Clinton is elected President, winning support from 47 percent of the female voters versus 41 percent of male voters. Democrat Carol Moseley Braun of Illinois is the first black woman elected to the Senate.

More than 500,000 people demonstrate for women's reproductive rights in Washington, D.C. The U.S. Supreme Court rules to uphold Roe v. Wade.

Astronaut Shannon Lucid

October is designated "Breast Cancer Awareness Month."

'93

President Clinton signs the Family and Medical Leave Act into law and lifts restrictions on abortion counseling and fetal-tissue research.

Ladies' Home Journal exposes the plight of baby girls in China as a result of the "one child" rule by publishing "Please Let Me Have My Baby," the story of a Chinese woman who fled to the United States to have her child.

The United Nations Commission on Human Rights condemns gender-based human rights violations.

Lieutenant Jeanne Flynn becomes the first female Air Force fighter pilot.

Janet Reno becomes the first female U.S. Attorney General; other women appointed to top posts in the new Clinton administration include Donna Shalala as Secretary of Health and Human Services; Alice Rivlin as deputy director of the Office of Management and Budget; Madeleine Albright as

U.S. ambassador to the United Nations; and Pamela Harriman as U.S. ambassador to France. The Ms. Foundation for Women sponsors "Take Our Daughters to Work Day."

'94

The indictment of O.J. Simpson for the murder of his ex-wife Nicole Brown Simpson focuses national attention on the problem of spousal abuse.

Ladies' Home Journal publishes "What's Wrong With Our Children?," a story about the mysterious incidence of higher birth defects born to veterans of the Gulf War.

A vote from U.S. bishops and Vatican approval allows altar girls to serve at mass for the first time.

The Wonderbra debuts in America and is promoted as "a safe alternative to breast implants—the look without the surgery."

Celebrities and breast cancer awareness

Players in the Women's National Basketball Association

For the first time editors of all "Seven Sisters" women's service magazines—Ladies' Home Journal, Good Housekeeping, Family Circle, Redbook, Woman's Day, McCall's, and Better Homes and Gardens— are women.

'95

The United Nations' Fourth World Conference on Women meets in Beijing, China, and is attended by 30,000 women, including First Lady Hillary Rodham Clinton, who leads the American delegation

Shannon Faulkner, 20, wins her two-year legal fight to gain admission to the cadet corps of the Citadel, an unaffiliated military academy in Charleston, South Carolina. She drops out after five days due to exhaustion during "Hell Week" boot camp.

'96

The Citadel military academy admits four women. A few months later, two resign, saying that they have been assaulted and sexually harassed.

Astronaut Shannon Lucid ends a 188-day stay in space, the longest by any American and by a woman.

'97

Ladies' Home Journal conducts the American Woman Survey, the first major study to examine the changes in women's lives over the past 30 years.

Two popular diet drugs, fen fluramine and dexfenfluramine (fen-fen), are removed from the market at the FDA's request after they are found to cause heart ailments. The drugs are reportedly used by 600,000 Americans.

The Women's National Basketball Association (WNBA) finishes its first season with the Houston Comets defeating the New York Liberty, 65–51.

One of the McCaughey septuplets

Bobbi McCaughey, a 29-year-old Iowan, gives birth to the world's only surviving septuptlets. The births give rise to safety and ethical questions regarding multiple births resulting from fertility treatments.

Carol Moseley Braun

Ellen De Generes, star of the television situation comedy series Ellen, reveals to Time magazine that she is gay. Her character on the series comes out of the closet at the same time, becoming the first openly gay leading character in a network series.

'98

At the Winter Olympics in Japan, women's hockey is a medal sport for the first time, with the U.S. women's team winning the gold medal.

Viagra, a drug that treats male impotence, is approved by the FDA and marketed by Pfizer.

Picture Credits

Research by Carousel Research, Inc.

The following abbreviations are used:
A=Archive Photos
AH=American Heritage
AP=AP/Wide World
B=UPI/Corbis-Bettmann
C=Culver Pictures
G=Gamma Liaison
LPW=Laurie Platt Winfrey, Inc.
P=Photofest
PR=Photo Researchers
All pictures are listed left to right clockwise by page.

Cover
First Row: Dias/Sipa; Everett Collection; C.S. Bull/Kobal Collection; Bernard Gotfryd/Woodfin Camp **Second Row:** A, Kim Knott/Camera Press/Retna; A **Third Row:** Raphael Wodman/G; A/American Stock **Fourth Row:** Francois Lochon/G; Lori Borgman/G; Kobal Collection; C; B

Introduction Pages
Page 2: C; B; B; B **3:** Paul S. Howell/G; Granger Collection; C; Thierry Falise/G **6:** Cecil Beaton/Camera Press/Globe; B; A **7:** A; B; A; B **8:** George Holz **12:** David Bartolomi

Activists & Politicians
14: Ed Clark/*Life* Magazine © Time Inc.; Francois Lochon/G; C; Jehangir Gazdar/Woodfin Camp; B **15:** Reuters/Peter Morgan/A **16:** Wallace Kirkland, Rapho/PR **17:** LPW; Private Collection **18:** Reuters/Jim Hollander/A **19:** R. Ellis/Sygma **20:** Granger Collection **21:** C; AH **22:** B; Reuters/Peter Morgan/A **23:** AP **24:** A **24/25:** Jehangir Gazdar/Woodfin Camp **25:** Hulton Getty **26:** Chris Kleponis/Woodfin Camp **27:** C; Holzworth Collection, Davidson Library, U.C. Santa Barbara **28/29:** Robert Trippett/Sipa **29:** Brad Markel/G **30:** George Ballis/Take Stock **31:** Betty Lane/PR **32:** Shlomo Arad/Woodfin Camp **33:** Micha Bar'Am/Magnum **34:** Paul S. Howell/G **35:** Supreme Court Historical Society **36:** Ed Clark/*Life* Magazine © Time Inc.; Bernard Gotfryd/Woodfin Camp; Everett Collection; Reuters/B **37:** B **38:** B **39:** Granger Collection; George Dabrowski/A **40:** Granger Collection **41:** C; C **42:** A **42/43:** Popperfoto/A **43:** Popperfoto/A; Raphael Wodman/G; Raphael Wodman/G **44/45:** PR **46:** Granger Collection **47:** A; AH; P; B **48:** Susan McElhinney/Woodfin Camp **49:** A; LPW **50/51:** Thierry Falise/G **51:** Yades/Sipa; Reuters/Apichart Weerawong/A **52:** Jehangir Gazdar/Woodfin Camp **53:** Ken Heyman/Woodfin Camp; Francois Lochon/G **54:** Brad Markel/G; Fraser/Sipa **55:** Dias/Sipa

Writers & Journalists
56: A; Globe; B; Lilly Library, Indiana University; A **57&58:** Chester Higgins, Jr./PR **59:** B; LPW **60:** A; Private Collection **61:** P **62/63:** A **63:** C, P **65:** Gisele Freund/PR **66:** Granger Collection; A; Granger Collection; Benelux/Sipa **67:** B **68:** LPW; Globe **69:** Schlesinger Library, Radcliffe College **70:** Elliott Erwitt/Magnum **71:** Ken Heyman/Woodfin Camp **72:** C; LPW **73:** Jan Collsi/G **74:** A **75:** Lilly Library, Indiana University **76:** Private Collection **77:** Granger Collection © 1998 Estate of Pablo Picasso/ARS, NY **78:** AP; ABC (2) **79:** Granger Collection; Collection of Jennifer Slegg **80:** Woolf/Bloomsbury/Hogarth Press Collection, Victoria University Library © 1961 Estate of Vanessa Bell; A **81:** Kobal Collection

Doctors & Scientists
82: B; B; Courtesy Helen Caldicott; Wellcome Institute Library **83:** Granger Collection **84:** Elizabeth Wilcox, Courtesy Special Collections, Columbia University Health Sciences Library **85:** Courtesy Helen Caldicott **86:** JL Charmet/SPL/PR **87:** Granger Collection **88:** SPL/PR **89:** Michael K. Nichols/National Geographic Society **90:** B **91:** Wellcome Institute Library (2) **92/93:** B **93:** John Reader/SPL/PR **94:** B **95:** B **96:** AH; Baldwin H. Ward/B **96/97** B

Entrepreneurs
98: Hulton Getty; Jason Trigg/A; Courtesy Jean Nidetch; A **99:** Catherine Karnow/Woodfin Camp **100/101:** A **101:** A; LPW **102:** P **103:** B; LPW **104:** Catherine Karnow/Woodfin Camp **105:** B; Mattel (2) **106:** Hulton Getty **107:** Courtesy Jean Nidetch **108:** Hulton Getty **109:** Globe **110:** Everett Collection **112:** Everett Collection; Jason Triggs/A **113:** Terry Thompson/Sipa

Artists & Entertainers
114: A; B; A; Kobal Collection; Cecil Beaton/Camera Press/Globe **115:** Granger Collection **116:** Ernest Sisto/NY Times Co./A **117:** B **118:** Kobal Collection **119:** P **120:** AP **121:** Margaret Bourke-White *Life* Magazine © Time Inc **122:** Cecil Beaton/Camera Press/Globe **123:** C; LPW **124:** C **125:** LPW **126:** P **127:** C.S. Bull/Kobal Collection **128:** C; A **129:** National Archives **130:** P **131:** A/American Stock; C.S. Bull/Kobal Collection; P; C; C **132:** Granger Collection **133:** Russell Reif/A **134:** A **135:** Schalkwijk/Art Resource, Instituto Nacional de Bellas Artes, Museo Dolores Olmedo Patiño; Sotheby's/Sipa, Instituto Nacional de Bellas Artes, Museo Dolores Olmedo Patiño **136:** Granger Collection **137:** A/Express Newspapers **138:** A; A; P; Kobal Collection **139:** Kobal Collection **140:** Art Resource © Georgia O'Keeffe Foundation/ARS, NY; Granger Collection **141:** Yousuf Karsh/Woodfin Camp **142:** Kobal Collection **143:** Leni Riefenstahl-Produktion

Athletes
144: A; B; B; Brown Brothers **145:** B **146:** G; G **147:** G; Depardon Uzan/G **148/149** B **149:** Brown Brothers; Brown Brothers; B; Brown Brothers; B **150:** B **151:** A **152:** Granger Collection **153:** B **154:** B **155:** B

Pioneers & Adventurers
156: Courtesy Susan G. Komen Foundation; A; Kim Knott/Camera Press/Retna; A **157:** Lori Borgman/G **158:** Courtesy Susan G. Komen Foundation **159:** Abolafia/G; Sophia Smith Collection, Smith College **160:** Jane Fincher/G; Reuters/Jose Manuel Ribeiro/A **161:** Kim Knott/Camera Press/Retna **162/163:** B **163:** Lori Borgman/G **164:** A **165:** A **166:** Popperfoto/A **167:** Luc Novovitch/G **168:** A **169:** B **170:** A; Sovfoto/Eastfoto

Timeline
172: P; MCNY/A; A; C; LPW; Minnesota Historical Society; Ford Archives; Popperfoto/A **173:** LPW; A; Granger Collection; LPW **174:** Library of Congress; NYPL; C; Granger Collection; C; Library of Congress **175:** Granger Collection; A; A; Granger Collection; LPW **176:** LPW; LPW; Minnesota Historical Society; LPW; B; C **177:** A; Granger Collection; Granger Collection; Granger Collection **178:** Granger Collection; A/*Paris Match*; LPW; Hurrell/Chapman College/A; Grumman Corporation; National Archives; Michael Barson/A **179:** LPW; B; B; Brown Brothers; Granger Collection; B **180:** A/Express Newspapers; Lambert/A; Ray Ellis/ Science Source/PR; A; B; B **181:** LPW; Frank Edwards/Fotos International/A; Frank Edwards/Fotos International/A; A; *Ladies' Home Journal*; P **182:** B; Peter Keegan/A; B; B; P; AP **183:** Dan Coleman/A; Frans Rombout/Petit Format/PR; A; Gabriel/Explorer/PR; John Carter/PR **184:** Reuters/Gary Hershorn/A; Reuters/Mike Blake/A; *Ladies' Home Journal*; NASA/LPW **185:** Reuters/Jeff Topping/A; Reuters/Blank Children's Hospital/A; Consolidated News Pictures/Ron Sachs/A; Will & Deni McIntyre/PR; Reuters/Peter Morgan/A; Reuters/George Shelton/A

Back cover
A; Chester Higgins, Jr./PR; Globe; C; A/Express Newspapers; Granger Collection

index

C

D

100♀

100 ♀